THE BURGER

AN ACTION PACKED DELICIOUS ADVENTURE

LOVE FOOD™

First published in 2012

LOVE FOOD is an imprint of Parragon Books Ltd

Parragon
Queen Street House
4 Queen Street
Bath BA1 1HE, UK

www.parragon.com/lovefood

ISBN: 978-1-4454-7513-4

Printed in China

New Photography by Mike Cooper
New Food Styling by Lincoln Jefferson
New Recipes and Introduction by Tara Duggan
Cover and Internal Design by Lexi L'Esteve
Project Managed by Kerry Starr

Notes for the Reader
This book uses standard kitchen measuring spoons and cups. All spoon and cup measurements
are level unless otherwise indicated. Unless otherwise stated, milk is assumed to be whole, eggs
are large, individual vegetables are medium, and pepper is freshly ground black pepper. Unless
otherwise stated, all root vegetables should be washed and peeled before using.

Garnishes and serving suggestions are all optional and not necessarily included in the recipe
ingredients or method. The times given are only an approximate guide. Preparation times differ
according to the techniques used by different people and the cooking times may also vary from
those given. Optional ingredients, variations, or serving suggestions have not been included in
the calculations.

Recipes using raw or very lightly cooked eggs should be avoided by infants, the elderly, pregnant
women, and people with weakened immune systems. Pregnant and breast-feeding women are
advised to avoid eating peanuts and peanut products. People with nut allergies should be aware
that some of the prepared ingredients used in the recipes in this book may contain nuts. Always
check the packaging before use.

Picture acknowledgments
A Cheeseburger © Judy Unger/Getty Images (front cover)
Raw Burgers with Freshly Ground Pepper © Linda Lewis/Getty Images (page 9)
Ingredients for Burgers © Leigh Beisch/Getty Images (page 9)

THE BURGER

CONTENTS

THE HISTORY OF THE BURGER

NOT SURPRISINGLY, MORE THAN ONE PERSON HAS TAKEN CREDIT FOR INVENTING THE HAMBURGER. WHILE HUMANS HAVE BEEN EATING GROUND BEEF PATTIES FOR CENTURIES, THE TERM "HAMBURGER STEAK" STARTED POPPING UP IN THE UNITED STATES IN THE 1800S, SUPPOSEDLY NAMED FOR THE GERMAN IMMIGRANTS WHO ORDERED THEM IN RESTAURANTS. HOWEVER, THE QUESTION OF WHO STARTED PUTTING THESE GROUND BEEF "STEAKS" BETWEEN SLICES OF BREAD IS WHERE THE CONTROVERSY LIES.

IT MIGHT HAVE BEEN IN 1885, AT A COUNTY FAIR IN SEYMOUR, WISCONSIN, WHERE CHARLES NAGREEN SERVED HAMBURGER STEAKS BETWEEN PIECES OF BREAD FOR EASE OF CARRYING. OR IT COULD HAVE BEEN IN 1892 AT ANOTHER COUNTY FAIR IN AKRON, OHIO, WHEN FRANK MENSCHES WAS SAID TO RUN OUT OF SAUSAGE AND DECIDED TO GROUND FRESH BEEF FOR SANDWICHES INSTEAD. THE THIRD THEORY IS THAT LOUIS LASSEN INVENTED THE BURGER IN HIS SMALL DINER IN NEW HAVEN, CONNECTICUT, AT AROUND THE SAME TIME.

HAMBURGERS SPREAD IN POPULARITY IN THE FIRST HALF OF THE TWENTIETH CENTURY, PROLIFERATING IN CHAIN RESTAURANTS THROUGHOUT SOUTHERN CALIFORNIA, AND HAVE LONG SINCE BECOME A SYMBOL OF THE AMERICAN DIET. TODAY, THEY SEEM TO BE POPULAR EVERYWHERE, SUCH AS IN AUSTRALIA, WHERE PEOPLE LOVE TO TOP THEIR BURGERS WITH PICKLED BEETS, AND SOMETIMES EVEN WITH A FRIED EGG AND PINEAPPLE (SEE PAGE 126). IN KOREA, THE SPICY FERMENTED CABBAGE KNOWN AS KIMCHI GOES ON TOP OF BURGERS (SEE PAGE 140), AND IN JAPAN, BENTO BURGERS FEATURE BUNS MADE OF COMPRESSED RICE (SEE PAGE 138).

POULTRY, FISH, AND VEGETARIAN VERSIONS OF THE CLASSIC HAMBURGER ARE NOW THE NORM, AND EVEN FOUR-STAR CHEFS HAVE EMBRACED BURGERS, STUFFING THEM WITH FOIE GRAS AND TRUFFLES OR SIMPLY USING THE HIGHEST-GRADE MEATS AND SERVING THEM WITH HOMEMADE CONDIMENTS. THIS BASIC AMERICAN FOODSTUFF NOW HAS PERMUTATIONS, HIGH AND LOW, IN ALMOST EVERY CORNER OF THE GLOBE.

EQUIPMENT

TRUE TO ITS HUMBLE ORIGINS, THE BEEF BURGER IS A LOW-TECH FOOD REQUIRING NOT MUCH MORE THAN A SHARP KNIFE FOR SLICING TOMATOES AND A SKILLET, BROILER, OR BARBECUE. HERE IS THE ONLY EQUIPMENT YOU'LL REALLY NEED.

· Mixing bowls

· Spatula for flipping burgers

· Knives for slicing tomatoes (serrated works well), lettuce, and other condiments

· Balloon whisk for making sauces, such as mayonnaise

· Skillet or ridged grill pan: Look for heavy pans, which are better at transferring heat, to create a better sear on your burgers

· Broiler pan and rack

· Gas or charcoal barbecue

· Meat grinder or food processor (optional) to make the freshly ground Steakhouse Burger (see page 92)

KA-POW!

HOW TO MAKE THE PERFECT BURGER PATTY

Burgers are incredibly easy to prepare, and the only really important step, beyond not overcooking them, is forming the patty. The main thing to avoid is overworking the meat, which can result in tough instead of tender, juicy burgers.

Fresh ground beef is the easiest to work with, because it's both dry enough and sticky enough to bind well. Ground turkey, chicken, and pork can be much wetter than beef and, therefore, harder to shape, but adding some bread crumbs can help alleviate that problem. Wetting your hands while forming the patties will also help. The same applies to vegetarian burgers, which can be wet and difficult to shape.

To form patties, place the meat in a bowl, add all of the seasonings at once, then mix—preferably with your hands—just until the seasonings are fully integrated.

Divide the meat into portions, then gently form each portion into even-size patties. If possible, make the patties slightly wider than the buns, because they will shrink during cooking. For the same reason, it also helps to make the edges of the patty thicker than the center, or to add a dimple to the center of the patty, so that when the meat contracts, the patty will end up an even thickness.

Quick cooking methods with high, dry heat are the best way to get burgers nicely browned on the outside while keeping them juicy inside.

Fried and Grilled
This is the classic diner method, which involves a hot skillet or ridged grill pan and some cooking fat. The burgers cook over medium-high heat until they develop a golden brown crust.

Steamed
Steaming takes frying one step further to keep the meat extra-moist. While frying, just cover the burgers with a lid to finish cooking.

Barbecued
Charcoal barbecues provide a smoky flavor, but gas ones are easier to use. To check the heat level of your barbecue after preheating, hold your hand about 1 inch above the cooking grate. The time it takes to get uncomfortably hot determines how hot the grill is:

high: about 3 seconds
medium-high: about 5 seconds
medium: about 7 seconds

Smoked
An aluminum foil pouch of wood chips creates smoke that melds its flavor into burgers cooking in a covered barbecue (see page 94). Different kinds of wood create different flavors, so experiment. Smoking on a barbecue requires a barbecue with a lid or hood.

Broiled
Broiling is an easier, low-mess method that works especially well for fish, poultry, or vegetarian burgers, which tend to stick to the grill grate. It is also a great alternative for any recipe that calls for a barbecue when the weather doesn't say "outdoor cooking."

HINTS AND TIPS

Choose meat with the right amount of fat. Burgers cook over a relatively high heat, so using lean meat can result in dry burgers. The preferred fat amount for beef is 18-22 percent, such as ground chuck, and ground turkey or chicken from leg meat is the best choice for poultry burgers when it comes to flavor and texture.

YOU CAN GRIND ALMOST ANY KIND OF FRESH MEAT YOURSELF. BEYOND THE STEAKHOUSE BURGERS (SEE PAGE 92), WHICH ARE MADE WITH BEEF, YOU CAN USE THE SAME METHOD WITH CHICKEN, LAMB, PORK, OR TURKEY. JUST CUT THE MEAT INTO 1-INCH CUBES AND CHILL FIRST TO AVOID ENDING UP WITH PUREED MEAT (THIS IS PARTICULARLY IMPORTANT WITH POULTRY).

BE GENTLE WITH THE MEAT. IF YOUR BURGERS COME OUT A LITTLE TOUGH, IT MEANS THAT YOU PROBABLY HANDLED THE MEAT TOO MUCH WHEN FORMING THE PATTIES.

If you prefer your burgers well done, add grated cheese or finely chopped vegetables to the meat to keep it moist. Some people even add chipped ice to their ground meat, around 2 crushed ice cubes per 1 pound of meat (these would need to be cooked immediately, for obvious reasons).

CHOOSE YOUR BUNS WISELY. MOST BURGER AFICIONADOS PREFER SOFTER BUNS OR BREAD THAT DOESN'T FIGHT WITH THE MEAT OR VEGETABLE PATTY. IF YOU LIKE TO WARM THE BUNS, DON'T ALLOW THEM TO GET TOO DRY AND TOASTY, WITH A FEW EXCEPTIONS, SUCH AS THE PATTY MELTS (SEE PAGE 56).

Preheat. Whether using a skillet, broiler, or barbecue, make sure the cooking surface or grill is hot before you add the burgers. This will prevent them from sticking and result in the best browning.

Don't mess with the burgers. Some cooks like to flip their burgers several times and can't help but press down on them with a spatula. This will only toughen them up.

If your burger isn't binding—this can be a problem especially with poultry, fish, or vegetarian burgers—try adding bread crumbs to the mixture. Chill the formed burgers for 15 minutes to help them stay together.

A FEW RECIPES CALL FOR AN ITEM ON THE BARBECUE TO BE COVERED. IN THESE CASES, IT IS BEST TO USE A BARBECUE THAT HAS A FITTED LID OR HOOD. ULTIMATELY, THIS FEATURE ENABLES AN INTENSE SMOKY FLAVOR TO PENETRATE THE FOOD AND ALSO GUARANTEES MORE EVEN COOKING. A BARBECUE WITH A LID OR HOOD IS ESPECIALLY RECOMMENDED FOR PULLED PORK BURGERS (SEE PAGE 66) AND SMOKED BURGERS (SEE PAGE 94).

CHAPTER 1
THE TIMELESS
ORIGINALS

THE TRADITIONAL HAMBURGER

PREP TIME: *15 minutes, plus chilling*   **COOK TIME:** *20 minutes*

NO BARBECUE IS COMPLETE WITHOUT THE CLASSIC HAMBURGER. THESE ARE SEASONED WITH ONION, GARLIC, AND MUSTARD, BUT YOU CAN MAKE THEM IN THE PURE TRADITION OF BEEF, SALT, AND PEPPER, IF YOU PREFER.

MAKES 4–6

1 pound fresh ground chuck beef

1 onion, grated

2–4 garlic cloves, crushed

2 teaspoons whole-grain mustard

2 tablespoons sunflower oil

pepper

4–6 hamburger buns, halved

Homemade Ketchup (see page 170)

Fries, to serve (see page 206)

FRIED ONIONS

2 tablespoons olive oil

4 onions, finely sliced

2 teaspoons light brown sugar

1. Preheat the grill. Place the ground beef, onion, garlic, mustard, and pepper in a large bowl and mix together thoroughly, squeezing the meat with your hand. Shape into four to six equal patties, then cover and let chill in the refrigerator for 30 minutes.

2. Meanwhile, make the fried onions. Heat the olive oil in a heavy skillet, add the onions, and sauté over low heat until soft. Add the sugar and cook for an additional 8 minutes, stirring occasionally, or until the onions have caramelized. Drain well on paper towels and keep warm.

3. To cook the burgers on the grill, check they are firm and brush generously with oil. Cook for about 5 minutes on each side, or until cooked to your liking. Place the hamburger buns on the preheated grill, cut side down, until lightly toasted. Place the burgers in the buns and top with the onions. Serve immediately with ketchup and fries.

REMEMBER TO COOK VEGETARIAN FOOD ON A SEPARATE GRILL AWAY FROM MEAT AND FISH, WHICH CAN SPIT AND GET ONTO THE FOOD IF COOKED NEARBY.

THE BEST CHEESEBURGER

PREP TIME: 10 minutes   **COOK TIME:** 12 minutes

MAKES 4

1½ pounds fresh
ground beef

1 beef bouillon cube

1 tablespoon ground
dried onion

2 tablespoons water

1-2 tablespoons
sunflower oil

½ cup shredded
American or
cheddar cheese

lettuce leaves

4 hamburger buns,
halved

tomato slices

Fries, to serve
(see page 206)

1. Place the beef in a large mixing bowl. Crumble the bouillon cube over the meat, add the dried onion and water, and mix well. Divide the meat into four equal portions, shape each into a ball, then flatten slightly to make a patty of your preferred thickness.

2. Place a ridged grill pan or skillet over medium-high heat. Lightly brush the burgers with oil and cook for 5-6 minutes. Turn the burgers, sprinkle the cheese over the cooked side, and cook for an additional 5-6 minutes, or until cooked to your liking.

3. Place the lettuce leaves on the bottom halves of the buns and top with the burgers. Place a couple of tomato slices on top and add the lids. Serve immediately with fries.

STEP 1

STEP 2

STEP 3

FOR AN EXTRA SPICY KICK TO THIS CLASSIC CHEESEBURGER, PLACE A GOOD SPOONFUL OF ENGLISH MUSTARD ON TOP OF THE COOKED BURGER BEFORE ADDING THE CHEESE.

TOFU BURGER

PREP TIME: 15 minutes, plus marinating   **COOK TIME:** 6 minutes

A STANDARD 8-OUNCE PACKAGE OF TOFU MAKES ENOUGH FOR ABOUT THREE BURGERS, BUT YOU CAN EASILY DOUBLE THE RECIPE.

MAKES 3

8 ounces firm tofu

2 tablespoons soy sauce

1/2 teaspoon Worcestershire sauce

1 garlic clove, minced

1/4 teaspoon crushed red pepper

8 small fresh cilantro sprigs, coarsely chopped

1/4 cup mayonnaise

3 hamburger buns, halved

red onion slices

lettuce leaves

1. Preheat the broiler to high and place the rack about 6 inches below the heat. Line the broiler pan with aluminum foil.

2. Drain the tofu and pat dry. Slice into 1/2-inch thick slabs that will roughly fit in the buns and drain on paper towels.

3. Combine the soy sauce, Worcestershire sauce, half the garlic, and the crushed red pepper in a shallow dish wide enough to fit the tofu in a single layer. Place the tofu in the mixture, then turn to coat on both sides. Place in the refrigerator and marinate for at least 15 minutes or for up to 3 hours.

4. Put the cilantro and the remaining garlic into a small food processor or blender and puree. Add the mayonnaise and mix until smooth.

5. Transfer the tofu to the prepared broiler pan. Cook under the preheated broiler for 3 minutes on each side, or until brown.

6. Spread the cilantro-garlic mayonnaise on both halves of the buns, then add one-third of the tofu to each of the bun bottoms. Add some onion and lettuce, finish with the top halves of the buns, slice in half, and serve immediately.

STEP 5

STEP 3

TOFU IS MADE FROM SOYBEANS. IT HAS LITTLE FLAVOR OF ITS OWN, BUT IT WILL EASILY ABSORB ANY FLAVORS OF THE INGREDIENTS IT IS COMBINED WITH. IT IS AN EXCELLENT SOURCE OF PROTEIN AND IS IDEAL FOR VEGETARIANS.

BACON CHEESEBURGER

PREP TIME: *15 minutes*   **COOK TIME:** *less than 20 minutes*

THIS DINER STANDBY FEATURES THE HARD-TO-BEAT COMBINATION OF BEEF, BACON, AND CHEESE.

MAKES 4

6 bacon strips

1 pound fresh ground beef

American or Swiss cheese slices

4 hamburger buns, halved

2 tablespoons mayonnaise

lettuce leaves

tomato slices

salt and pepper

1. Preheat the grill to medium-high. Put the bacon in a skillet over medium heat and cook for about 8 minutes, or until crisp. Drain on paper towels and break the strips in half.

2. Put the beef in a bowl and season with the salt and pepper. Divide into four equal portions and shape each portion into a patty.

3. Place the patties on the grill and cook, covered, for 4 minutes. Turn, top each burger with a slice of cheese, replace the cover, and cook for an additional 4 minutes, or until the burgers are cooked to your liking and the cheese is melted.

4. Spread both halves of the buns with mayonnaise, then place each burger on a bun bottom. Top with the bacon pieces, lettuce, and tomato slices, then finish with the top halves of the buns. Serve immediately.

If you like your burgers with a little spicy kick, why not add some homemade chipotle ketchup (see page 180)

OUR FAMOUS TURKEY BURGER

PREP TIME: 10 minutes   COOK TIME: 5 minutes

LOW IN FAT BUT PACKED FULL OF FLAVOR, TURKEY BURGERS MAKE A DELIGHTFUL CHANGE FROM THEIR BEEFY COUSINS AND WILL BE POPULAR WITH ALL THE FAMILY.

MAKES 4

12 ounces fresh ground turkey

¼ cup fresh whole-wheat bread crumbs

1 small onion, finely chopped

1 apple, such as McIntosh, peeled, cored, and finely chopped

grated rind and juice of 1 small lemon

2 tablespoons finely chopped fresh parsley

sunflower oil, for brushing

salt and pepper

4 whole-grain sandwich buns or focaccia, halved

1. Preheat the broiler to medium—high and line the broiler pan with aluminum foil. Place the turkey, bread crumbs, onion, apple, lemon rind and juice, and parsley into a large bowl. Season with salt and pepper and gently mix to combine. Divide into four equal portions and shape each portion into a patty.

2. Brush the patties with oil and place on the prepared pan. Cook, turning once, for 5 minutes, or until cooked through. To test the burgers, pierce them with the tip of a sharp knife; if the juices run clear, they are ready. If there are any traces of pink, return them to the broiler for 1-2 minutes.

3. Place a burger on each bun bottom, add the bun lids, and serve immediately.

STEP 2

STEP 1

These burgers are slightly more fragile than burgers made with beef, so handle them with care when placing them on the broiler pan and when turning them.

23

THE CLASSIC CHICKEN BURGER

PREP TIME: 15–20 minutes, plus chilling

COOK TIME: 15–20 minutes

MAKES 4

4 large skinless, boneless chicken breasts

1 extra-large egg white

1 tablespoon cornstarch

1 tablespoon all-purpose flour

1 egg, beaten

1¼ cups fresh white bread crumbs

2 tablespoons sunflower oil

beefsteak tomato slices

4 hamburger buns, halved

shredded lettuce leaves

mayonnaise

Fries, to serve (see page 206)

1. Place the chicken breasts between two sheets of nonstick parchment paper and flatten slightly using a meat mallet or a rolling pin. Beat together the egg white and cornstarch, then brush the mixture over the chicken. Cover and let chill in the refrigerator for 30 minutes, then coat in the flour.

2. Place the egg and bread crumbs in two separate bowls and coat the chicken first in the egg, letting any excess drip back into the bowl, then in the bread crumbs.

3. Heat a heavy skillet and add the oil. When hot, add the chicken and cook over medium heat for 6–8 minutes on each side, or until thoroughly cooked. Add the tomato slices for the last 1–2 minutes of the cooking time to heat through.

4. Place the chicken in the hamburger buns with the tomato slices, a little shredded lettuce, and a spoonful of mayonnaise. Serve immediately with fries.

THIS CLASSIC BURGER IS A FIRM
FAVORITE WITH CHICKEN AND
BURGER ENTHUSIASTS ALIKE,
AND FOR THOSE WHO LIKE TO
WATCH WHAT THEY EAT, CHICKEN
BURGERS ARE LOWER IN FAT
THAN THE TYPICAL BEEF TYPE.

THE ULTIMATE VEGGIE BURGER

PREP TIME: 10 minutes, plus chilling

COOK TIME: 35 minutes

MAKES 4–6

½ cup brown rice

1 (15-ounce) can great Northern beans, drained and rinsed

1 cup unsalted cashew nuts

3 garlic cloves

1 red onion, cut into wedges

¾ cup corn kernels

2 tablespoons tomato paste

1 tablespoon chopped fresh oregano

2 tablespoons whole-wheat flour

2 tablespoons sunflower oil

salt and pepper

shredded lettuce leaves

4–6 whole-wheat buns, halved

tomato slices

Muenster cheese slices

1. Cook the rice in a saucepan of lightly salted boiling water for 20 minutes, or according to the package directions, until tender. Drain and place in a food processor or blender.

2. Add the beans, cashew nuts, garlic, onion, corn, tomato paste, oregano, and salt and pepper to the rice in the food processor and, using the pulse button, blend together. Shape into four to six equal patties, then coat in the flour. Cover and let chill in the refrigerator for 1 hour.

3. Preheat the grill. Brush the patties with the oil and cook over medium-hot coals for 5-6 minutes on each side, or until cooked through.

4. Place the shredded lettuce leaves on the bottom halves of the buns and top with the burgers. Top each with one or two tomato slices and a cheese slice. Place under a hot broiler, or put on the grill and cover, for 2 minutes, until the cheese begins to melt. Add the bun lids and serve immediately.

THIS IS A FANTASTIC BURGER FOR BOTH VEGETARIANS AND NONVEGETARIANS, FULL OF FLAVOR, TEXTURE, AND HEALTHY INGREDIENTS. YOU CAN, IF YOU LIKE, USE BLACK-EYED PEAS OR RED KIDNEY BEANS INSTEAD OF THE GREAT NORTHERN BEANS.

THE EVERYTHING BURGER

PREP TIME: 15 minutes   **COOK TIME:** less than 10 minutes

THIS CHEESEBURGER INCLUDES JALAPEÑO CHILES AND COLESLAW ALONG WITH SOME OF THE OTHER TRADITIONAL BURGER CONDIMENTS.

MAKES 4

1 pound fresh ground beef
1 teaspoon salt
½ teaspoon pepper
vegetable oil, for frying
Monterey Jack or American cheese slices
4 soft hamburger buns, halved
mustard, for spreading
Pickled Jalapeños (see page 198)
Coleslaw (see page 176)
tomato slices

1. Put the ground beef into a medium bowl with the salt and pepper and gently mix to combine, then divide into four equal portions and shape each portion into a patty.

2. Place a large skillet or griddle pan over medium-high heat and add enough oil to coat the bottom of the skillet. Add the patties, partly cover, and cook for about 4 minutes, without moving, until the burgers are brown and come away easily from the skillet. Turn, place a slice of cheese on top of each burger, partly cover again, and cook for an additional 3 minutes, or until cooked to your liking.

3. Spread the mustard on both halves of the buns and place a few slices of pickled jalapeños on each bun bottom. Set a burger on top of each bottom, add some coleslaw and a tomato slice, and serve immediately.

YOU CAN ADD AS LITTLE OR
AS MUCH AS YOU LIKE TO THIS
ALL-AMERICAN BURGER.
FOR SOMETHING A LITTLE
DIFFERENT, WHY NOT TRY
HOMEMADE CHIPOTLE MUSTARD
(SEE PAGE 180)

DOUBLE-DECKER BURGER

PREP TIME: *20 minutes*   **COOK TIME:** *less than 10 minutes*

ALSO CALLED A "DOUBLE" AT FAST-FOOD RESTAURANTS, A DOUBLE-DECKER STACKS TWO BEEF PATTIES FOR A HUGE MOUTHFUL OF A BURGER.

MAKES 4

2 pounds fresh ground beef
2 teaspoons salt
½ teaspoon pepper
vegetable oil, for frying
Swiss, American, or Cheddar cheese slices
4 soft hamburger buns, halved
lettuce leaves
tomato slices
red onion slices
pickles, halved lengthwise

1. Place the beef in a medium bowl with the salt and pepper and mix gently to combine. Divide into eight equal portions and shape each portion into a patty no thicker than ½ inch—the thinner the better for these burgers.

2. Place a large, ridged grill pan or skillet over medium-high heat. Add enough oil to coat the bottom of the pan. Add the patties and cook for about 4 minutes, without moving, until the burgers are brown and come away easily from the pan. Turn and cook on the other side for 2 minutes, then put a slice of cheese on top of each burger and cook for an additional 2 minutes, or until cooked to your liking.

3. Place a burger on each bun bottom, then place a second burger on top. Add the lettuce leaves, tomato slices, onion slices, and pickles and serve immediately.

STEP 1

STEP 2

TO MAKE THIS BURGER MORE MANAGEABLE, MAKE SURE THAT THE PATTIES ARE NOT TOO BIG OR TOO THICK.

BLUE CHEESE & ONION BURGER

PREP TIME: 15 minutes   **COOK TIME:** less than 10 minutes

A CROWN OF MELTING BLUE CHEESE AND RED ONION RINGS MAKE THIS BURGER DISTINCTIVE.

MAKES 4

1 pound fresh ground beef

1 teaspoon salt

½ teaspoon pepper

vegetable oil, for brushing

4 hamburger buns, halved

½ cup crumbled blue cheese

lettuce leaves

red onion slices

1. Preheat the broiler to high. Place the broiler rack 2-3¼ inches below the heat.

2. Put the ground beef into a medium bowl with the salt and pepper and mix gently to combine, then divide into four equal portions and shape each portion into a patty.

3. Brush the patties with oil, place on the rack, and cook for about 4 minutes on each side, or until cooked to your liking.

4. Place the burgers in the buns. Put some cheese on top of each burger, pressing it down slightly to hold its shape. Top with the lettuce and onions and serve immediately.

STEP 2

STEP 3

STEP 4

BLUE CHEESE HAS A DISTINCTIVE LOOK AND SMELL AND CAN ALSO VARY CONSIDERABLY IN STRENGTH.

MUSHROOM-SWISS BURGER

PREP TIME: 30 minutes   COOK TIME: 15 minutes

IT'S HARD TO BEAT THE CLASSIC COMBINATION OF
SAUTÉED MUSHROOMS AND SWISS CHEESE ON TOP OF A
GRILLED BURGER.

MAKES 4

2 teaspoons vegetable oil, plus extra for brushing

½ yellow onion, thinly sliced

1½ cups sliced button mushrooms

1 pound fresh ground beef

1 teaspoon salt

½ teaspoon pepper

Swiss cheese slices

4 poppy seed buns, halved

lettuce leaves

tomato slices

salt and pepper

1. Heat the oil in a medium skillet over medium-high heat. Add the onion and cook for 3 minutes, stirring, until soft. Add the mushrooms and season with salt and pepper. Cook for 1-2 minutes, then stir. Continue to cook until the mushrooms are cooked through.

2. Place the beef in a bowl, add the 1 teaspoon salt and ½ teaspoon pepper, and gently mix to combine. Divide into four equal portions and shape each portion into a patty.

3. Heat a ridged grill pan or skillet over medium-high heat, then brush with oil. Add the patties and cover the pan. Cook for about 4 minutes, until brown, then turn and cook on the other side for 2 minutes. Add the cheese and cook for an additional 2 minutes, or until cooked to your liking.

4. Place the lettuce and tomato slices on each bun bottom. Add the cheese patties then the mushroom mixture and the top halves of the buns. Serve immediately.

STEP 1

STEP 3

MAKE SURE YOU COOK
THE MUSHROOMS IN A
LARGE ENOUGH PAN
SO THAT THEY ARE
BROWNED INSTEAD OF
BEING STEAMED.

CHILI BURGER

PREP TIME: 15 minutes   **COOK TIME:** less than 10 minutes

THIS BEEF EXTRAVAGANZA OF A BURGER SMOTHERED IN BEEF CHILI AND CHEESE ORIGINALLY CAME FROM LOS ANGELES DINERS.

MAKES 4

1 pound fresh ground beef
1 teaspoon salt
½ teaspoon pepper
1 tablespoon butter
4 soft hamburger buns, halved
½ quantity Beef Chili (see page 194), warmed
red onion slices
¼–½ cup shredded cheddar cheese

1. Put the ground beef into a medium bowl, add the salt and pepper, and mix gently to combine. Divide into four equal portions and shape each portion into a patty.

2. Heat a large skillet over medium-high heat. Melt the butter in the skillet and heat until it has stopped foaming. Add the patties and cook for about 4 minutes, without moving, until they are brown and come away easily from the skillet. Turn and cook on the other side for an additional 4 minutes, or until cooked to your liking.

3. Place the open buns on plates. Set each burger on a bun and ladle just enough beef chili on top to cover, then sprinkle with the onion and cheese. Serve immediately.

KA-POW!

THIS IS ONE BURGER YOU MAY NEED TO EAT WITH A FORK!

CARAMELIZED ONION BURGER

PREP TIME: *15 minutes* **COOK TIME:** *less than 15 minutes*

ROSEMARY-SCENTED BURGERS GET DRESSED UP WITH SILKY CARAMELIZED ONIONS, FOCACCIA, AND SHARP MANCHEGO CHEESE.

MAKES 4

1 pound fresh ground beef

1 teaspoon salt

½ teaspoon pepper

½ teaspoon finely chopped fresh rosemary

vegetable oil, for frying

½–¾ cup shredded manchego cheese or manchego cheese slices

½ cup mayonnaise

4 pieces focaccia, about 6 x 6 inches and halved

Caramelized Onions (see page 202)

romaine lettuce leaves

tomato slices

1. Place the ground beef in a medium bowl with the salt, pepper, and rosemary and gently mix to combine, then divide into four equal portions and shape each portion into a patty.

2. Place a large skillet or griddle pan over medium-high heat. Add enough oil to coat the bottom of the skillet. Add the patties and cook for about 4 minutes, without moving, until the burgers are brown and come away easily from the pan. Turn and cook for 2 minutes, then place some cheese on top of each burger and cook for an additional 2 minutes, or until cooked to your liking.

3. Spread the mayonnaise on the focaccia. Place the burgers on the bottom pieces of the foccacia, top with the caramelized onions, lettuce leaves, and tomato slices, add the lids, and serve immediately.

STEP 2

STEP 2

STEP 3

FOCACCIA—A FLAT OVEN-
BAKED ITALIAN BREAD—MAKES
A DELICIOUS ALTERNATIVE TO
THE CLASSIC HAMBURGER BUN.

SLOPPY JOES

PREP TIME: 10 minutes   COOK TIME: 1 hour

THE SECRET TO A GREAT SLOPPY JOE IS SLOWLY SIMMERING THE BEEF MIXTURE UNTIL IT'S RICH AND TENDER. BY THE WAY, YOU SHOULD ALWAYS SERVE SLOPPY JOES WITH A FORK, BUT YOU SHOULD NEVER NEED TO USE IT!

MAKES 4—6

1½ pounds fresh ground beef

½ onion, diced

2 garlic cloves, minced

1 green bell pepper, seeded and diced

2 cups water

¾ cup ketchup

1½ tablespoons light brown sugar

1 teaspoon Dijon mustard

dash of Worcestershire sauce

1½ teaspoons salt

½ teaspoon black pepper

cayenne pepper, to taste

4-6 hamburger buns, halved

potato chips, to serve (optional)

1. Put the ground beef and onions into a large cold skillet and place over medium heat. Cook, stirring, breaking up the meat into small pieces with a wooden spoon, until it begins to brown.

2. Add the garlic and green bell pepper and cook, stirring, for 2 minutes. Add half the water. Cook until simmering, scraping up any sediment from the bottom of the pan.

3. Stir in the ketchup, sugar, mustard, Worcestershire sauce, salt, black pepper, cayenne pepper, and the remaining water. Bring to simmering point, reduce the heat to low, and simmer for 30-45 minutes, or until most of the liquid has evaporated and the meat mixture is thick, rich, and tender. Spoon the beef mixture onto each bun bottom. Add the bun lids and serve immediately with potato chips, if desired.

These burgers are always served hot, but the sloppy joe mixture can be made in advance and reheated. Make double the quantity — it can be frozen for up to three months.

BEAN BURGER

PREP TIME: *15 minutes*   **COOK TIME:** *10-12 minutes*

MAKES 4

1 (15-ounce) can red kidney beans, drained and rinsed

1 (15-ounce) can chickpeas, drained and rinsed

1 egg yolk

¼ teaspoon smoked paprika

1 cup fresh bread crumbs

3 scallions, finely chopped

oil for brushing

salt and pepper

4 crusty bread rolls, halved

lettuce leaves

tomato slices

4 tbsp sour cream

1. Preheat the grill to high.

2. Place the beans, chickpeas, egg yolk, paprika, bread crumbs, and scallions in a large bowl and gently mix to combine. Season with salt and pepper. Divide the mixture into four equal portions and shape each portion into a patty. Season the outside of the patties with salt and pepper and lightly brush with oil.

3. Oil the grill grate. Cook the burgers for 5 minutes on each side, or until cooked through. Brush the inside of the buns with oil and toast over the grill, cut side down, for 1-2 minutes. Place some lettuce and tomatoes on each bun bottom. Add the burgers and top with sour cream and the bun lids. Serve immediately.

IF THE BURGERS DO NOT HOLD TOGETHER WHEN YOU TRY TO SHAPE THEM, ADD JUST A LITTLE MORE OIL TO THE MIXTURE TO MAKE THEM EASIER TO HANDLE.

43

BARBECUE BURGER

PREP TIME: *15 minutes*   **COOK TIME:** *less than 10 minutes*

THIS SIMPLE BURGER FEATURES BARBECUE SAUCE; FOR EVEN MORE AUTHENTIC FLAVOR, TRY SMOKING YOUR BURGERS (SEE PAGE 94).

MAKES 4

1 pound fresh ground beef

1 teaspoon salt

½ teaspoon pepper

¼ cup finely chopped onion

1 garlic clove, minced

¾ cup Barbecue Sauce (see page 172)

4 soft hamburger buns, halved

lettuce leaves

tomato slices

1. Preheat the grill to medium-high. Put the ground beef into a medium bowl with the salt, pepper, onion, and garlic and mix gently to combine. Divide into four equal portions and shape each portion into a patty.

2. Place ½ cup of the barbecue sauce in a bowl.

3. Put the patties on the grill and cook for 4 minutes, until brown on one side. Turn, baste with the barbecue sauce, and cook for an additional 4 minutes, until cooked to your liking.

4. Spread some of the remaining barbecue sauce on the buns, then place the burgers on the bun bottoms. Top with the lettuce leaves and tomato slices, add the bun lids, and serve immediately.

STEP 1

STEP 3

STEP 3

IF YOU DON'T HAVE THE TIME TO MAKE YOUR OWN BARBECUE SAUCE, THERE ARE MANY EXCELLENT STORE-BOUGHT VERSIONS YOU CAN TRY.

45

TURKEY CLUB BURGER

PREP TIME: 20 minutes   **COOK TIME:** 20 minutes

TAKING A CUE FROM CLUB SANDWICHES—STACKS OF SLICED TURKEY WITH BACON, LETTUCE, AND TOMATO BETWEEN TOASTED BREAD—THESE BURGERS ARE LAYERED WITH FLAVOR.

MAKES 4

1 pound fresh ground turkey

1 garlic clove, minced

1½ teaspoons finely chopped fresh rosemary

1 teaspoon salt

½ teaspoon pepper

6 bacon strips

8 sourdough, rye, or white sandwich bread slices, toasted

2–3 tablespoons ranch-style dressing

lettuce leaves

tomato slices

1. Preheat the grill to medium-high. Combine the ground turkey with the garlic, rosemary, salt, and pepper in a bowl. Divide the mixture into four equal portions and shape each portion into a thick patty.

2. Cook the bacon in a skillet over medium heat for about 8 minutes, or until crisp. Drain on paper towels and break the pieces in half.

3. Spread each slice of bread with about ½ teaspoon of the ranch-style dressing.

4. Put the patties on the grill and cook over medium heat, covered, for 4-5 minutes on each side, or until cooked through.

5. Place each burger on a slice of the toasted bread, add the bacon, lettuce leaves, and tomato slices, drizzle with a little more dressing, and top with the remaining toasted bread. Serve immediately.

STEP 1

STEP 3

THE CREAMY RANCH-STYLE DRESSING IS THE PERFECT ACCOMPANIMENT FOR THIS TASTY BURGER. TRY USING IT AS A DIPPING SAUCE AS WELL—IT GOES PARTICULARLY WELL WITH FRIES!

THE BUTTER BURGER

PREP TIME: 30 minutes, plus chilling   **COOK TIME: 10 minutes**

THESE BURGERS CAN BE MADE WITH PLAIN BUTTER, BUT ARE BROUGHT TO A WHOLE NEW LEVEL WITH A LITTLE GARLIC AND PLENTY OF HERBS.

MAKES 4

5 tablespoons butter

1/2 teaspoon minced garlic

1 tablespoon finely chopped fresh parsley

1 teaspoon finely chopped fresh thyme, rosemary and/or sage

1 1/2 teaspoons salt

1 pound fresh ground beef

4 soft hamburger buns, halved

1. Put 4 tablespoons of the butter into a small bowl with the garlic, herbs, and 1/2 teaspoon of the salt and gently mix to combine. Transfer the butter mixture to a piece of plastic wrap and roll into a 1-inch thick log. Chill in the refrigerator for at least 1 hour and up to 2 days.

2. When ready to make the burgers, remove the butter log from the refrigerator, cut into four equal slices, and set aside to return to room temperature.

3. Combine the ground beef and the remaining salt in a large bowl. Divide into four equal portions and shape each portion into a patty.

4. Heat a large skillet over medium-high heat. Add the remaining butter and heat until foaming. When it has stopped foaming add the burgers and cook for about 4 minutes, without moving, until the burgers are brown and come away easily from the pan. Turn and cook for an additional 4 minutes on the other side, or until cooked to your liking.

5. Place a burger on each bun bottom. Top with the seasoned butter, add the bun lids, and serve immediately.

You can vary the herbs used in your butter mixture to your liking. Parsley, oregano, chives, basil, and tarragon all work well, or add a little fresh red chile for a spicier version.

49

LAMB BURGER

PREP TIME: 10 minutes, plus chilling   **COOK TIME:** 20-25 minutes

MAKES 4-6

2 tablespoons olive oil

1 red bell pepper, seeded and cut into quarters

1 yellow bell pepper, seeded and cut into quarters

1 red onion, cut into thick wedges

1 baby eggplant, cut into wedges

1 pound fresh ground lamb

2 tablespoons freshly grated Parmesan cheese

1 tablespoon chopped fresh mint

salt and pepper

4-6 hamburger buns, halved

shredded lettuce leaves

grilled vegetables, such as bell peppers and cherry tomatoes, to serve

MINTY MUSTARD MAYONNAISE

¼ cup mayonnaise

1 teaspoon Dijon mustard

1 tablespoon chopped fresh mint

1. Preheat the grill to medium-hot. Oil the grill grate.

2. Place the bell peppers, onions, and eggplant on the grill and cook over hot coals for 10-12 minutes, or until charred. Remove, let cool, then peel the peppers.

3. Place all the vegetables in a food processor or blender and, using the pulse button, chop. Add the ground lamb, Parmesan cheese, and chopped mint to the food processor, season with salt and pepper, and blend until combined. Divide the mixture into balls and flatten into patties about 1 inch thick. Season the outside with salt and pepper, and lightly brush with oil.

4. Next, make the minty mustard mayonnaise. Blend the mayonnaise with the mustard and chopped fresh mint. Cover and chill in the refrigerator until required.

5. Place the burgers over hot coals and cook for 5 minutes on each side, or until cooked through. Brush the inside of the buns with oil and toast over the grill, cut side down, for 1-2 minutes. Place the shredded lettuce on the bun bottoms, top with the burgers, spread some of the prepared mayonnaise on top of the burgers, and add the lids. Serve immediately with the grilled vegetables on the side.

LAMB AND FRESH MINT ARE A
CLASSIC PARTNERSHIP, WHICH IS
GREATLY ENHANCED HERE BY THE
INTRODUCTION OF SWEET BELL
PEPPERS, RICH EGGPLANT,
AND A LITTLE PUNGENT
PARMESAN CHEESE.

BACON-WRAPPED CHICKEN BURGER

PREP TIME: *10 minutes, plus chilling*

COOK TIME: *10-15 minutes*

MAKES 4

1 pound fresh ground chicken

1 onion, grated

2 garlic cloves, crushed

⅓ cup pine nuts, toasted

½ cup shredded Swiss or Gruyère cheese

2 tablespoons fresh snipped chives

2 tablespoons whole-wheat flour

8 strips bacon

1-2 tablespoons sunflower oil

salt and pepper

4 crusty rolls, halved

red onion slices

lettuce leaves

mayonnaise

scallions, chopped

1. Place the ground chicken, onion, garlic, pine nuts, cheese, chives, and salt and pepper in a food processor or blender. Using the pulse button, blend together the mixture using short, quick bursts. Scrape out onto a board and shape into four equal patties. Coat in the flour, then cover and chill in the refrigerator for 1 hour.

2. Wrap each patty with two bacon strips, securing in place with a wooden toothpick.

3. Heat a heavy skillet and add the oil. When hot, add the patties and cook over medium heat for 5-6 minutes on each side, or until cooked through.

4. Serve the burgers in the crusty rolls with the red onion, lettuce, a spoonful of mayonnaise, and scallions. Serve immediately.

You can alter the flavor and texture of these luxurious burgers by replacing the pine nuts with slivered almonds or unsalted cashew nuts. If using whole nuts, first chop them and, if desired, toast lightly.

53

SLOPPER BURGER

PREP TIME: *20 minutes, plus chilling*   **COOK TIME:** *45 minutes*

DARK GREEN POBLANO CHILES ARE COMMON IN THE PUEBLO AND COLORADO SPRINGS AREA OF COLORADO. THE DARKER THE CHILE, THE RICHER ITS FLAVOR WILL BE.

MAKES 4

8 poblano chiles
2 onions
3 garlic cloves
1 tablespoon vegetable oil
1½ teaspoons salt
2 pounds fresh ground beef
Monterey Jack or cheddar cheese slices
4 hamburger buns, halved

1. Preheat the grill to high. Place the chiles on the grill and cook, turning occasionally, until the skin is blackened. Set aside for about 15 minutes, or until cool enough to handle.

2. Meanwhile, finely chop the onions and garlic. Peel and chop the chiles.

3. Put the oil, three-quarters of the chopped onion, and ½ teaspoon of the salt into a medium saucepan over high heat and cook, stirring frequently, for about 3 minutes, or until soft. Add the garlic and chiles, cover, reduce the heat to low, and cook for about 30 minutes, or until the flavors have blended and the vegetables are all soft. Set aside.

4. Place the ground beef and the remaining salt in a large bowl and gently mix to combine. Divide into four equal portions and shape each portion into a patty. Cover and chill in the refrigerator.

5. Place the buns cut side down on the grill and toast for 1–2 minutes. Transfer the buns to plates.

6. Place the patties on the grill and cook for about 4 minutes, until brown, then flip and cook on the other side. After 2 minutes, put a slice of cheese on top of each burger, cover, and cook for about 3 minutes, or until the burgers are cooked to your liking and the cheese is melted.

7. Place a burger on each bun bottom. Top with the green chili sauce and the remaining chopped onion, add the bun lids, and serve immediately.

STEP 6

STEP 1

POBLANO CHILES CAN BE FOUND IN MEXICAN STORES AND SOME SUPERMARKETS, PARTICULARLY IN THE SOUTHWEST. HOWEVER, YOU CAN ALSO USE ANY CHILE OF YOUR CHOICE — JUST REMEMBER THAT CHILES CAN VARY GREATLY IN BOTH SIZE AND HEAT!

PATTY MELT

PREP TIME: 20 minutes   COOK TIME: 12 minutes

A PATTY MELT TAKES TWO CLASSIC SANDWICHES—BURGER AND GRILLED CHEESE—AND PUTS THEM TOGETHER WITH RYE BREAD AND CARAMELIZED ONIONS.

MAKES 4

2 tablespoons softened butter, plus extra for greasing

8 light rye bread slices

8 Swiss, American, or cheddar cheese slices

1¼ pounds fresh ground beef

1 teaspoon salt

½ teaspoon pepper

1 quantity Caramelized Onions (see page 202)

1. Spread the butter on the bread. Place four slices, buttered side down, on a clean work surface. Top each slice with one slice of cheese.

2. Put the beef into a bowl, add the salt and pepper, and combine. Divide into four equal portions and shape each portion into a rectangular patty.

3. Grease a griddle pan or skillet with butter and heat over medium heat. Add the patties to the pan and cook for about 4 minutes on each side, or until cooked to your liking. Wipe the pan clean.

4. Place the patties on top of the cheese-topped bread slices, then add the caramelized onions and the remaining cheese slices. Top with the remaining bread slices, buttered side up.

5. Place the sandwiches in the wiped pan and cook over medium heat for 2 minutes on each side, or until golden brown. Serve immediately.

CHEESE AND ONION IS A WELL-KNOWN AND DELICIOUS COMBINATION OF INGREDIENTS. YOU CAN BUY CARAMELIZED ONIONS FROM MOST GOOD SUPERMARKETS AND ALSO VARY THE CHEESE USED TO SUIT YOUR TASTES.

THE CLASSIC FISH BURGER

PREP TIME: *10 minutes*   **COOK TIME:** *10 minutes*

THIS FISH BURGER IS A CLASSIC ON HAWAIIAN MENUS, WHERE IT IS OFTEN MADE WITH MAHI MAHI (A.K.A. DORADO). OTHER WHITE FISH, SUCH AS POLLACK OR TILAPIA, WORK PERFECTLY WHEN MAHI MAHI ISN'T AVAILABLE.

MAKES 4

4 mahi mahi or other white fish fillets, about 4-6 ounces each

2 teaspoons vegetable or canola oil

½ teaspoon sea salt

¼ teaspoon pepper

4 soft hamburger buns, halved

¼ cup Tartar Sauce (see page 182)

onion slices

tomato slices

lettuce leaves

1. Rinse the fish and pat dry. Rub the fillets on both sides with the oil and sprinkle with the salt and pepper. Place on a large baking sheet.

2. Preheat the broiler to high and place the rack about 3¼ inches below the heat.

3. Place the fish on the rack and cook under the preheated broiler for 4 minutes, then turn and cook for an additional 3 minutes, or until the edges start to brown and the fish is just cooked through (the center of the fish should flake easily when cut into).

4. Spread each bun bottom with tartar sauce, add the fish and top with onion and tomato slices and some lettuce leaves. Add the bun lids and serve immediately.

STEP 4

STEP 4

FOR A HAWAIIAN FEEL, TOP THESE BURGERS WITH SOME JUICY PINEAPPLE SLICES.

THE JUICY LUCY BURGER

PREP TIME: *20 minutes*   **COOK TIME:** *15–25 minutes*

A CULT HIT IN MINNESOTA, THESE CHEESE-STUFFED BURGERS ARE BIG ENOUGH TO ACCOMMODATE THE FILLING. BE CAREFUL BECAUSE THE MOLTEN FILLING WILL BE VERY HOT WHEN THE BURGERS COME OFF THE GRILL.

MAKES 2

12 ounces fresh ground beef
1 teaspoon salt
½ teaspoon pepper
2 American cheese slices, quartered
vegetable oil, for frying
½ red onion, sliced
2 soft hamburger buns, halved
lettuce leaves
tomato slices

1. Preheat the grill to medium-high. Put the ground beef in a small bowl with the salt and pepper and combine. Divide into four equal portions and roll each portion into a ball. Place the balls on a clean work surface and flatten until slightly larger than the buns and about ½ inch thick. Arrange the cheese in a circle on top of two of the patties, leaving a ½-inch border. Add the second patty and firmly press the sides to seal (otherwise the cheese will come out during cooking).

2. Heat the oil in a skillet over medium heat. Add the onion slices and sauté for about 8 minutes, stirring frequently, until soft and brown. Alternatively, you could grill the onion slices for about 2 minutes on each side while you cook the burgers.

3. Place the patties on the grill, rounded side up. Cook for 8 minutes, then carefully turn over and cook on the other side for 5-7 minutes.

4. Place each burger on a bun bottom, top with the onions, lettuce, tomatoes, and the top half of the bun, and serve immediately.

STEP 1

STEP 2

You can use any cheese you desire in this recipe. To make it even more indulgent, try adding some fried bacon pieces with the cheese in the center of the burgers.

BURGER LETTUCE WRAP

PREP TIME: 15 minutes   **COOK TIME:** less than 10 minutes

THESE FRESH BURGERS HAVE NO BUNS OR CHEESE TO GET IN THE WAY OF THE MEAT. THE CRISP, JUICY VEGETABLES OFFSET THE BEEF'S RICH FLAVOR AS IT COMES OFF THE GRILL.

MAKES 4

1 pound fresh ground beef

1/4 teaspoon dried thyme or 1/2 teaspoon chopped fresh thyme

zucchini slices

vegetable oil, for brushing

lettuce leaves

tomato slices

onion slices

salt and pepper

1. Preheat the grill to medium-high. Put the ground beef into a medium bowl with 1/2 teaspoon of salt, 1/4 teaspoon of pepper, and the thyme. Gently mix to combine, then divide into four equal portions and shape each portion into a patty.

2. Lightly brush the zucchini slices with oil and sprinkle with salt and pepper.

3. Place the patties and zucchini slices on the grill. Cook the zucchini slices for about 3 minutes on each side, until soft and marked. Cook the burgers for 4 minutes on each side, or until cooked to your liking.

4. Place a burger on a few lettuce leaves. Top with the zucchini, tomato, and onion slices, then wrap the lettuce over to encase the burger. Serve immediately.

THIS BURGER IS PERFECT IF YOU ARE TRYING TO CUT DOWN ON CARBOHYDRATES IN YOUR DIET BECAUSE IT'S COMPLETELY BREAD-FREE!

CHAPTER 2
THE GOURMET
SHOWSTOPPERS

PULLED PORK BURGER

PREP TIME: *20 minutes, plus standing*   **COOK TIME:** *6 hours*

SLOW-COOKED PORK "PULLED" INTO SHREDS AND TOPPED WITH SWEET-YET-VINEGARY SAUCE MAKES IRRESISTIBLE BURGERLIKE SANDWICHES.

SERVES 12

1 pork butt, about 5 pounds

¼ cup paprika

¼ cup firmly packed dark brown sugar

2 tablespoons salt

2 tablespoons pepper

2 tablespoons ground cumin

2 tablespoons dry mustard

1 tablespoon cayenne pepper

12 soft sandwich buns, halved

Homemade Pickle Relish (see page 178)

Barbecue Sauce (see page 172)

1. Prepare a grill with a lid for low-medium heat by building the fire on only one side (heat only one element on a gas barbecue), then place a saucepan filled halfway with water on the unlit side and set the grate over it.

2. Rinse the pork and pat dry. In a small bowl, mix the paprika, sugar, salt, pepper, cumin, mustard, and cayenne pepper. Rub this spice mixture all over the pork. Use all of the mixture, making a thin crust on the meat.

3. Place the pork on the grill over the pan of water. Cover the grill with the lid, and cook for about 6 hours, until the meat is extremely tender. Check about every 30 minutes to make sure the fire is still going, adding more fuel and water as needed.

4. Remove the meat from the grill and let stand for 10-20 minutes. Use forks or tongs to pull the pork into shreds.

5. Serve the pulled pork on a platter with the buns, pickle relish, and barbecue sauce, letting everyone make their own burger.

STEP 3

STEP 2

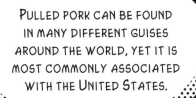

PULLED PORK CAN BE FOUND IN MANY DIFFERENT GUISES AROUND THE WORLD, YET IT IS MOST COMMONLY ASSOCIATED WITH THE UNITED STATES.

BLACK & BLUE BURGER

PREP TIME: *30 minutes*   **COOK TIME:** *10 minutes*

THESE BURGERS GET THEIR NAME FROM A BLACK PEPPER SPICE RUB AND A BLUE CHEESE DRESSING.

MAKES 4

4 ounces blue cheese
¼ cup mayonnaise
¼ cup sour cream
1 shallot, finely chopped
1 teaspoon pepper
1 teaspoon paprika
1 teaspoon dried thyme
1 teaspoon salt
½ teaspoon cayenne pepper
1 pound fresh ground beef
4 sesame seed hamburger buns, halved
lettuce leaves
tomato slices

1. Put the cheese, mayonnaise, and sour cream into a bowl and mash together until the mixture is as smooth as possible. Add the shallot and stir it into the dressing. Set aside.

2. Mix together the pepper, paprika, thyme, salt, and cayenne pepper in a small bowl.

3. Divide the meat into four equal portions and shape each portion into a patty. Sprinkle evenly on both sides with the spice mixture.

4. Heat a large, nonstick skillet over high heat. Add the patties and cook for about 4 minutes, until the spice mixture forms a light crust and the edges are brown. Turn and cook on the other side for an additional 4 minutes, or until brown and cooked to your liking.

5. Transfer the burgers to the buns, top with the blue cheese dressing, lettuce leaves, and tomato slices, and serve immediately.

STEP 1

STEP 2

STEP 4

You can vary the spices used in this recipe to suit your own personal tastes. Use garlic powder, onion powder, or even chili powder to give the spice rub a whole new dimension.

BEET BURGER

PREP TIME: 30 minutes, plus standing and chilling

COOK TIME: 35-40 minutes

THESE WHOLESOME, CRISP BEET-AND-MILLET BURGERS HAIL FROM AUSTRALIA. THE TANGY YOGURT SAUCE CONTRASTS WITH THE SWEET, EARTHY VEGETABLES.

MAKES 4

½ cup millet

¾ cup lightly salted water

1 cup grated raw beet (from 1-2 beets)

½ cup grated carrot

½ cup grated zucchini

½ cup finely chopped walnuts

2 tablespoons cider vinegar

2 tablespoons extra virgin olive oil, plus extra for frying

1 egg

2 tablespoons cornstarch

1 cup plain yogurt

2 teaspoons minced garlic

4 multigrain buns, halved

lettuce leaves

salt and pepper

1. Rinse and drain the millet, then put it into in a small saucepan with the salted water. Place over medium heat, bring to a simmer, cover, and cook over low heat for 20-25 minutes, until tender. Remove from the heat and let stand for 5 minutes, covered.

2. Put the beet, carrots, zucchini, and walnuts into a large bowl. Add the millet, vinegar, oil, ½ teaspoon of salt, and ¼ teaspoon of pepper and mix well. Add the egg and cornstarch, mix again, then chill in the refrigerator for 2 hours.

3. Put the yogurt in a fine strainer over a bowl and drain for at least 30 minutes. Stir in the garlic and season with salt and pepper.

4. Pack the beet mixture into a ½ cup measure, then shape into a patty. Repeat to make a total of four patties. Place a griddle or large skillet over medium heat and coat with oil. Add the patties and cook for about 5 minutes on each side, turning carefully, until brown.

5. Spread the buns with the yogurt sauce and place the burgers in the buns, topped with the lettuce. Serve immediately.

USE SMALLER BEETS WITH A DEEP MAROON COLORING BECAUSE THEY HAVE A SWEETER TASTE AND ARE MUCH MORE TENDER. LARGER BEETS CAN OFTEN BE WOODY WITH A TOUGH CENTER.

PORK BURGER

PREP TIME: *25 minutes, plus chilling*   **COOK TIME:** *45 minutes*

MAKES 4-6

1 pound pork tenderloin, cut into small pieces

3 tablespoons orange marmalade

2 tablespoons orange juice

1 tablespoon balsamic vinegar

2 parsnips (about 8 ounces), cut into chunks

1 tablespoon finely grated orange rind

2 garlic cloves, crushed

6 scallions, finely chopped

1 zucchini, shredded

1 tablespoon sunflower oil

salt and pepper

lettuce leaves

4-6 hamburger buns, halved

1. Place the pork in a shallow dish. Place the marmalade, orange juice, and vinegar in a small saucepan and heat, stirring, until the marmalade is runny. Pour the marinade over the pork. Cover and let stand for at least 30 minutes. Remove the pork, reserving the marinade. Grind the pork into a large bowl.

2. Meanwhile, cook the parsnips in a saucepan of boiling water for 15-20 minutes, or until tender. Drain, then mash and add to the pork. Stir in the orange rind, garlic, scallions, and zucchini, and season with salt and pepper. Mix together, then shape into four to six equal patties. Cover and let chill in the refrigerator for at least 30 minutes.

3. Preheat the grill. Lightly brush each patty with the oil and then add them to the grill, cooking over medium-hot coals for 4-6 minutes on each side, or until cooked through. Boil the reserved marinade for at least 5 minutes, then pour into a small bowl.

4. Place the lettuce leaves on the bottom halves of the hamburger buns and top with the burgers. Spoon over a little of the hot marinade, then top with the lids and serve immediately.

KA-POW!

THE PIQUANT FLAVOR OF ORANGE JUICE AND RIND IS THE MAKING OF THIS BURGER. EVEN THE LARGE PIECES OF ORANGE PEEL IN THE MARMALADE PLAY THEIR PART BY ADDING EXTRA TEXTURE.

TUNA BURGER

PREP TIME: *15 minutes, plus chilling*   **COOK TIME:** *25-35 minutes*

FRESH TUNA, CHILE, AND MANGO ARE UNITED IN A TOTALLY MODERN BURGER. TUNA IS BEST EATEN SLIGHTLY PINK—IT CAN BE DRY IF OVERCOOKED. IT IS ALSO IMPORTANT THAT THE BURGERS ARE PIPING HOT BEFORE SERVING.

MAKES 4—6

1 large sweet potato (about 8 ounces), chopped

1 pound tuna steaks

6 scallions, finely chopped

1 zucchini, shredded

1 fresh red jalapeño chile, seeded and finely chopped

2 tablespoons mango chutney

1 tablespoon sunflower oil

salt

lettuce leaves

MANGO SALSA

1 large ripe mango, peeled and pitted

2 ripe tomatoes, finely chopped

1 fresh red jalapeño chile, seeded and finely chopped

1½-inch piece cucumber, finely diced

1 tablespoon chopped fresh cilantro

1-2 teaspoons honey

1. Cook the sweet potatoes in a saucepan of lightly salted, boiling water for 15-20 minutes, or until tender. Drain well, then mash and place in a food processor or blender. Cut the tuna into chunks and add to the potatoes.

2. Add the scallions, zucchini, chile, and mango chutney to the food processor and, using the pulse button, blend together. Shape into four to six equal patties, then cover and chill in the refrigerator for 1 hour.

3. Meanwhile make the salsa. Slice the mango, reserving 8-12 slices for serving. Finely chop the remainder, then mix with the tomatoes, chile, cucumber, cilantro, and honey. Mix well, then spoon into a small bowl. Cover and let stand for 30 minutes to let the flavors develop.

4. Preheat the grill. Brush the burgers lightly with the oil and cook over hot coals for 4-6 minutes on each side, or until piping hot. Serve immediately with the mango salsa, garnished with lettuce leaves and the reserved mango slices.

STEP 1

STEP 3

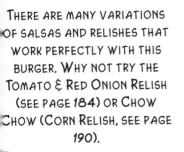

There are many variations of salsas and relishes that work perfectly with this burger. Why not try the Tomato & Red Onion Relish (see page 184) or Chow Chow (Corn Relish, see page 190).

CHEESE & APPLE BURGER

PREP TIME: 12 minutes, plus chilling   **COOK TIME:** 25–35 minutes

MAKES 4–6

4–6 new potatoes (about 6 ounces)

1½ cups mixed nuts, such as pecans, almonds, and hazelnuts

1 onion, coarsely chopped

2 small apples, such as McIntosh, peeled, cored, and grated

1½ cups crumbled blue cheese, such as Stilton

1¼ cups fresh whole-wheat bread crumbs

2 tablespoons whole-wheat flour

1–2 tablespoons sunflower oil

salt and pepper

lettuce leaves

4–6 cheese-topped hamburger buns, halved

red onion slices

1. Cook the potatoes in a saucepan of boiling water for 15–20 minutes, or until tender. Drain and, using a vegetable masher, crush into small pieces. Place in a large bowl.

2. Place the nuts and onion in a food processor or blender and, using the pulse button, chop finely. Add the nuts, onion, apple, cheese, and bread crumbs to the potatoes in the bowl. Season with salt and pepper. Mix well, then shape into four to six equal patties. Coat in the flour, then cover and let chill in the refrigerator for 1 hour.

3. Preheat the grill. Brush the patties with the oil and cook over medium coals for 5–6 minutes on each side, or until cooked through.

4. Place the lettuce leaves on the bottom halves of the buns and top with the burgers. Top with red onion slices, add the lids, and serve immediately.

BLUE CHEESE CAN HAVE A DOMINEERING FLAVOR, BUT NOT WHEN MIXED WITH APPLES AND NUTS IN A BURGER LIKE THIS. THESE ARE ALL REFRIGERATOR AND PANTRY INGREDIENTS, SO YOU CAN MAKE THIS RECIPE AT ANY TIME.

TURKEY & TARRAGON BURGER

PREP TIME: 20 minutes, plus chilling   COOK TIME: 20–30 minutes

WHAT A HEALTHY COMBINATION OF INGREDIENTS THERE IS IN THESE BURGERS. TURKEY AND TARRAGON CONTRIBUTE FINE, DISTINCTIVE FLAVORS, WHILE THE ROBUST BULGUR WHEAT IS THERE FOR ITS NUTTY TASTE AND COARSE TEXTURE.

MAKES 4

⅓ cup bulgur wheat
1 pound fresh ground turkey
1 tablespoon finely grated orange rind
1 red onion, finely chopped
1 yellow bell pepper, seeded, peeled, and finely chopped
¼ cup slivered almonds, toasted
1 tablespoon chopped fresh tarragon
1–2 tablespoons sunflower oil
salt and pepper
lettuce leaves
tomato relish
tomato and onion salad, to serve

1. Cook the bulgur wheat in a saucepan of lightly salted, boiling water for 10–15 minutes, or according to the package directions.

2. Drain the bulgur wheat, place in a bowl with the ground turkey, orange rind, onion, yellow bell pepper, almonds, and tarragon, and season with salt and pepper. Mix together, then shape into four equal patties. Cover and let chill in the refrigerator for 1 hour.

3. Preheat the grill. Brush the patties with the oil and cook over medium-hot coals for 5–6 minutes on each side, or until cooked through.

4. Put a few lettuce leaves on serving plates and place a burger on top of each, spoon a little relish over them, and serve immediately with a tomato and onion salad.

STEP 1

STEP 2

STEP 3

TARRAGON HAS A SLIGHT TASTE OF ANISE (WHICH HAS A SWEET LICORICE FLAVOR) AND IS THE PERFECT PARTNER TO TURKEY, CHICKEN, AND FISH.

SWEET POTATO & MUENSTER BURGER

PREP TIME: 10-12 minutes, plus chilling **COOK TIME: 40-45 minutes**

MAKES 4-6

3 sweet potatoes (about 1 pound), cut into chunks

2½ cups small broccoli florets

2-3 garlic cloves, crushed

1 red onion, finely chopped or grated

1½-2 fresh red jalapeño chiles, seeded and finely chopped

1½ cups shredded muenster cheese

2 tablespoons whole-wheat flour

2-3 tablespoons sunflower oil

4 onions, sliced

1 tablespoon chopped fresh cilantro

salt and pepper

1. Cook the sweet potato in a saucepan of lightly salted, boiling water for 15-20 minutes, or until tender. Drain and mash. Cook the broccoli in a separate saucepan of boiling water for 3 minutes, then drain and plunge into cold water. Drain again, then add to the mashed sweet potato.

2. Stir in the garlic, onion, chile, and cheese, and season with salt and pepper. Mix well and shape into four to six equal patties, then coat in the flour. Cover and let chill in the refrigerator for at least 1 hour.

3. Heat 1½ tablespoons of the oil in a heavy skillet. Add the onions and sauté over medium heat for 12-15 minutes, or until softened. Stir in the cilantro and reserve.

4. Preheat the grill. Brush the patties with the remaining oil and cook over medium coals for 5-6 minutes on each side, or until cooked through.

5. Top the burgers with the reserved fried onions and cilantro and serve immediately.

STEP 1

STEP 2

STEP 2

THERE ARE LOTS OF INTERESTING TEXTURES AND FLAVORS VYING FOR YOUR ATTENTION IN THESE TASTY BURGERS. FOR AN EXTRA CHEESY KICK, SHALLOW-FRY SOME SLICES OF HALLOUMI CHEESE TO SERVE ON TOP OF THE BURGERS.

BURGER TARTARE

PREP TIME: *20 minutes*   **COOK TIME:** *10 minutes*

DON'T WORRY, THESE AREN'T ACTUALLY RAW BURGERS.
INSTEAD, THEY USE THE TRADITIONAL ACCOMPANIMENTS
FOR STEAK TARTARE TO CREATE A REMARKABLY
JUICY BURGER.

MAKES 6

6 gherkin pickles

2 tablespoons capers

1 teaspoon pickled green peppercorns

2 egg yolks

1 teaspoon salt

1½ pounds fresh ground beef

6 hamburger buns or baguette-style buns, halved

6 tablespoons mayonnaise

1. Preheat the broiler to high. Place the rack 2-3¼ inches below the heat.

2. Meanwhile, finely chop the pickles, capers, and peppercorns.

3. Put the egg yolks into a large bowl and lightly beat. Stir in the pickles, capers, peppercorns, and salt. Add the beef and gently but thoroughly work in the egg mixture. Divide into six equal portions and shape each portion into a patty.

4. Lay the patties on a large baking sheet, place on the broiler rack, and cook under the preheated broiler for about 4 minutes, until they are sizzling and starting to brown. Turn and cook on the other side for about 4 minutes, or until the burgers are cooked to your liking.

5. Meanwhile, spread each bun with about 1 tablespoon of the mayonnaise. Place the burgers in the buns and serve immediately.

STEP 5

STEP 2

ADD A FEW DASHES OF
TABASCO SAUCE FOR THOSE
WHO LIKE THEIR FOOD SPICY.

SALMON BURGER

PREP TIME: *15 minutes, plus chilling* **COOK TIME:** *25–35 minutes*

MAKES 4–6

2–3 medium potatoes (about 10 ounces), cut into chunks

1 pound fresh salmon fillet, skinned

1 (6-ounce) package fresh spinach leaves

½ cup pine nuts, toasted

2 tablespoons finely grated lemon rind

1 tablespoon chopped fresh parsley

2 tablespoons whole-wheat flour

1 cup crème fraîche or plain Greek yogurt

1½-inch piece cucumber, peeled and finely chopped

2 tablespoons sunflower oil

salt and pepper

4–6 whole-wheat hamburger buns, halved

grilled cherry tomatoes, to serve

1. Cook the potatoes in a saucepan of lightly salted, boiling water for 15–20 minutes, or until tender. Drain well, then mash and reserve. Chop the salmon into chunks.

2. Reserve a few spinach leaves for serving, then blanch the remainder in a saucepan of boiling water for 2 minutes. Drain, squeezing out any excess moisture, then chop.

3. Place the spinach in a food processor or blender with the salmon, potatoes, pine nuts, 1 tablespoon of the lemon rind, and the parsley, and season with salt and pepper, then, using the pulse button, blend together. Shape into four to six equal patties, then cover and let chill in the refrigerator for 1 hour. Coat the patties in the flour.

4. Mix together the crème fraîche, cucumber, and the remaining lemon rind in a bowl, then cover and let chill until required.

5. Preheat the grill. Brush the patties with the oil and cook over medium-hot coals for 4–6 minutes on each side, or until cooked through.

6. Place the reserved spinach leaves on the bottom halves of the buns and top with the burgers, then spoon over a little of the crème fraîche mixture. Add the lids and serve immediately with grilled cherry tomatoes.

Fresh salmon, spinach, and pine nuts create a colorful burger. Be sure to squeeze as much water as possible out of the fresh spinach, otherwise the burgers may end up being soggy.

LEMON & MINT TURKEY BURGER

PREP TIME: *10 minutes, plus chilling*   **COOK TIME:** *15 minutes*

MAKES 6

1 pound fresh ground turkey

½ small onion, grated

finely grated rind and juice of 1 small lemon

1 garlic clove, minced

2 tablespoons finely chopped fresh mint

½ teaspoon pepper

1 teaspoon sea salt

1 egg, beaten

1 tablespoon olive oil

lemon wedges, to serve

1. Place all the ingredients except the oil in a bowl and mix well with a fork. Divide into 12 equal portions and shape each portion into a patty. Cover and chill in the refrigerator for at least 1 hour, or overnight.

2. Heat the oil in a large, heavy skillet. Add the burgers, cooking in batches, if necessary. Cook over medium-high heat for 4-5 minutes on each side, until golden brown and cooked through.

3. Transfer the burgers to a warm serving plate and serve immediately with the lemon wedges for squeezing over the burgers.

KA-POW!

Turkey meat is leaner than chicken and great for those who are conscious of their fat and calorie intake. Serve without bread and with roasted vegetables, instead of fries, for an ultrahealthy burger meal.

PASTRAMI BURGER

PREP TIME: *15 minutes*   **COOK TIME:** *10 minutes*

THE ORIGINS OF THESE OVER-THE-TOP BURGERS IS UNCLEAR, BUT SOMEHOW THEY HAVE TAKEN ROOT IN SALT LAKE CITY, UTAH.

MAKES 4

1 pound fresh ground beef

1 teaspoon salt

½ teaspoon pepper

1 tablespoon butter

Swiss or Gruyère cheese slices

4 sesame seed hamburger buns, halved

¼ cup store-bought Thousand Island dressing

shredded lettuce leaves

8 ounces pastrami slices

1. Put the ground beef into a medium bowl with the salt and pepper and mix gently to combine. Divide into four equal portions and shape each portion into a patty.

2 Heat a ridged grill pan or large skillet over medium-high heat. Add the butter and heat until it has stopped foaming. Add the patties and cook for about 4 minutes, without moving, until they are brown and come away easily from the pan. Turn and cook on the other side for 2 minutes, then put a slice of cheese on top of each burger and cook for an additional 3 minutes, until cooked to your liking.

3. Place the open buns on plates. Spread with the Thousand Island dressing, then place some shredded lettuce on each bun bottom. Set a burger on top, pile with the pastrami, and add the lid. Serve immediately.

STEP 1

STEP 2

STEP 2

COMBINE THIS DELICIOUS BURGER WITH SOME HOMEMADE MUSTARD (SEE PAGE 174), OR FOR AN ADDED KICK, SOME HOMEMADE CHIPOTLE MUSTARD (SEE PAGE 180).

MARYLAND CRAB CAKE BURGER

PREP TIME: 25 minutes, plus chilling   **COOK TIME:** less than 15 minutes

IN MARYLAND, EXTRA-LARGE CRAB CAKE SANDWICHES ARE OFTEN SERVED IN BUNS WITH LETTUCE AND TOMATOES, JUST LIKE BURGERS.

MAKES 6

1 pound crabmeat
2/3 cup mayonnaise
1 tablespoon chopped fresh parsley
1 teaspoon Old Bay seasoning or other seafood seasoning mix
1 egg
1 teaspoon Worcestershire sauce
1 teaspoon dry mustard
1/2 teaspoon salt
1/4 teaspoon pepper
1/3 cup dried bread crumbs
2 tablespoons butter
6 hamburger buns, halved
tomato slices
shredded lettuce leaves
Tartar Sauce (see page 182) and lemon wedges, to serve

1. Put the crabmeat into a medium bowl and add the mayonnaise, parsley, seasoning, egg, Worcestershire sauce, mustard, salt, and pepper. Gently mix, then add the bread crumbs, a little at a time, and mix gently until combined. Chill in the refrigerator for at least 30 minutes.

2. Divide the mixture into six equal portions and shape each portion into a patty.

3. Heat a ridged grill pan or skillet over medium heat, add the butter, and heat until no longer foaming, stirring to coat the bottom of the pan. Add the patties and cook for about 6-7 minutes on each side, until golden.

4. Put the burgers on the bun bottoms and top with the tomato slices, lettuce, and tartar sauce before adding the lids. Serve immediately with lemon wedges.

POW

You can buy old bay seasoning from the supermarket or make your own by grinding and combining a tablespoon each of celery seed, whole black peppercorns, and sweet paprika, half a teaspoon each of whole cardamom and mustard seeds, quarter a teaspoon of mace, 4 whole cloves, and 6 bay leaves.

STEAKHOUSE BURGER

PREP TIME: *20 minutes, plus chilling*   **COOK TIME:** *10 minutes*

THE VERY BEST BURGERS ARE MADE WITH FRESHLY CHOPPED MEAT, AND YOU DON'T NEED A MEAT GRINDER FOR THE TASK.

MAKES 4

1 pound boneless chuck roast, round, or boneless short ribs or a mixture with at least 20 percent fat

1 teaspoon salt

½ teaspoon pepper

4 hamburger buns, halved

Swiss cheese slices

2 tablespoons mayonnaise

2 tablespoons ketchup

lettuce leaves

tomato slices

1. Preheat the grill to medium-high. Chop the beef into 1-inch cubes, then place on a plate, wrap in plastic wrap, and chill in the refrigerator for about 30 minutes.

2. Place half the beef in a food processor or blender. Pulse (do not run the processor) about 15 times. Season the meat with half the salt and half the pepper, and pulse an additional 10-15 times, until the meat is finely chopped but not overprocessed. Remove from the processor and repeat with the remaining beef. Divide into four equal portions and shape each portion into a patty.

3. Place the patties on the grill and cook until brown and cooked to your liking, 3 minutes on each side for medium-rare and 4 minutes on each side for medium. Place a slice of cheese on each burger during the last 2 minutes of cooking.

4. Meanwhile, put the mayonnaise and ketchup into a small bowl and mix to combine. Spread on the buns, then add the burgers with the lettuce leaves and tomato slices. Serve immediately.

KA-POW!

STEP 1

STEP 2

STEP 4

FOR BURGERS THIS SPECIAL,
IT'S BEST TO COOK THEM ON THE
MEDIUM-RARE SIDE.

SMOKED BURGER

PREP TIME: *25 minutes*   **COOK TIME:** *10 minutes*

SLICED ONIONS, COOKED SLOWLY UNTIL GOLDEN BROWN AND SLIGHTLY SWEET, ARE A DELICIOUS ACCOMPANIMENT TO ALL KINDS OF BURGERS.

MAKES 4

wood chips, for smoking

1 pound fresh ground beef
1 teaspoon salt
½ teaspoon pepper
smoked Gouda cheese slices
brioche buns, halved

FIG RELISH

1 quantity Caramelized Onions (see page 202)
¼ cup fig preserves
1 tablespoon red wine vinegar
1 tablespoon soy sauce
1 teaspoon Worcestershire sauce
pepper

1. Soak the wood chips in water for at least 10 minutes.

2. To make the relish, put the caramelized onions, preserves, vinegar, soy sauce, Worcestershire sauce, and pepper to taste into a medium saucepan. Bring to low simmer and cook for 1-2 minutes, until it forms a thick relish. Set aside.

3. Put the ground beef in a bowl with the salt and pepper and gently mix to combine. Divide into four equal portions and shape each portion into a patty.

4. If using a gas barbecue grill, wrap the drained wood chips in aluminum foil, making a pouch but leaving the ends open to let the smoke escape. Lift the grate, place the pouch on top of a side burner, and turn the heat to high. Turn the other burners to medium or low, cover, and preheat the grill to 400°F.

5. If using a charcoal barbecue grill, preheat to medium-high. Push the coals to one side and place the wood chips on top.

6. When the wood starts smoking, put the patties on the grate on the opposite side of the grill. Cover and cook for about 4 minutes, until brown, then turn and cook on the other side. After 2 minutes, add the cheese and cook for an additional 2 minutes, or until the burgers are brown and cooked to your liking.

7. Place the burgers in the buns and top with some of the relish. Serve immediately.

STEP 6

STEP 3

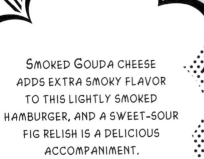

SMOKED GOUDA CHEESE ADDS EXTRA SMOKY FLAVOR TO THIS LIGHTLY SMOKED HAMBURGER, AND A SWEET-SOUR FIG RELISH IS A DELICIOUS ACCOMPANIMENT.

BLT BURGER WITH ASPARAGUS

PREP TIME: *12 minutes, plus chilling*   **COOK TIME:** *15 minutes*

MAKES 4-6

8 ounces bacon strips

1 pound fresh ground beef

1 onion, grated

2-4 garlic cloves, crushed

1-2 tablespoons sunflower oil

salt and pepper

lettuce leaves

4-6 hamburger buns, halved

tomato slices

DIP

6 ounces baby asparagus spears

1 tablespoon lemon juice

1 small ripe avocado, peeled, pitted, and finely chopped

2 firm tomatoes, peeled, seeded, and finely chopped

2/3 cup crème fraîche or Greek yogurt

salt and pepper

1. Remove any rind and fat from the bacon strips and chop finely.

2. Place the bacon, ground beef, onion, and garlic in a large bowl, season with salt and pepper, and mix well. Shape into four to six equal patties, then cover and let chill in the refrigerator for 30 minutes.

3. To make the dip, trim the asparagus and cook in a saucepan of lightly salted, boiling water for 5 minutes, then drain and plunge into cold water. When cold, drain and finely chop half the spears into a bowl and reserve the rest to serve. Sprinkle the lemon juice over the avocado. Stir in the avocado, tomatoes, and crème fraîche. Season with salt and pepper, cover, and let chill in the refrigerator until required.

4. Preheat the grill. Lightly brush the patties with the oil and cook over hot coals for 3-4 minutes on each side, or until cooked to your liking.

5. Place the lettuce leaves on the bottom halves of the buns and top with the burgers. Top with a tomato slice, an asparagus spear, and a spoonful of the dip. Add the lids and serve immediately.

WHAT COULD BE BETTER FOR FANS OF THE BLT THAN A BLT BURGER? THE ASPARAGUS AND AVOCADO DIP ADDS THAT EXTRA TASTE DIMENSION. WHEN MAKING DIPS OR SALSAS, PREPARE THEM AT LEAST 30 MINUTES BEFORE USING TO ALLOW TIME FOR THE FLAVORS TO DEVELOP.

BURGER WITH SAUTÉED MUSHROOMS

PREP TIME: *25 minutes*   **COOK TIME:** *25 minutes*

THE ADDITION OF SAUTÉED DICED MUSHROOMS
ADDS A NOTE OF COMPLEXITY TO THE BEEF
IN THESE DELICIOUS BURGERS.

MAKES 4

extra virgin olive oil, for frying

1 garlic clove, finely chopped

½ teaspoon finely chopped fresh rosemary or thyme

8 ounces button or cremini mushrooms, stems removed and finely chopped (about 3 cups)

1 pound fresh ground beef

Jarlsberg, Swiss, or cheddar cheese slices

½ teaspoon salt

¼ teaspoon pepper

4 brioche buns, halved

softened butter, for spreading

salt and pepper

1. Heat the oil in a large skillet over medium heat. Add the garlic and rosemary and sauté for 30 seconds, until fragrant. Add the mushrooms and stir for 1 minute, until well coated. Season with salt and pepper, then reduce the heat slightly and cook for an additional 15 minutes, stirring frequently, until the liquid evaporates and the mushrooms are tender and dry.

2. Place the mushrooms in a medium bowl and let cool, then add the ground beef, ½ teaspoon of salt, and ¼ teaspoon of pepper. Stir gently, then divide into 4 equal portions and shape each portion into a patty.

3. Return the skillet to medium-high heat. Add enough oil to coat the bottom of the skillet. Add the patties and cook for about 4 minutes, until they are brown and come away easily from the skillet. Turn and cook for 2 minutes, then place a slice of cheese on top of each burger and cook for an additional 2 minutes, or until cooked to your liking.

4. Spread the butter on the buns, add the burgers and bun lids, and serve immediately.

STEP 1

STEP 2

STEP 3

THIS SAUTÉED MUSHROOM MIXTURE IS COMMONLY KNOWN AS DUXELLES AND USED MOST NOTABLY IN BEEF WELLINGTON. ADD SHALLOTS FOR A MORE AUTHENTIC FLAVOR AND CREAM FOR A MORE LUXURIOUS VERSION.

TRUFFLE BURGER

PREP TIME: *10 minutes*   **COOK TIME:** *20 minutes*

THESE BURGERS ARE TOPPED WITH TRUFFLE OIL AND A PARMESAN CHIP AND ARE SERVED OPEN-FACED ON A PIECE OF FOCACCIA.

MAKES 4

1 pound fresh ground beef

2 cups freshly grated Parmesan cheese

½ teaspoon salt

½ teaspoon pepper

4 pieces of focaccia, 6 x 6 inches and halved

1 teaspoon white truffle oil

1. Preheat the broiler to high. In a large bowl, gently combine the beef, 2/3 cup of the cheese, and the salt and pepper. Divide the mixture into four equal portions and shape each portion into a patty. Place the patties on a baking sheet and set aside.

2. Heat a non-stick skillet over medium heat. Divide the remaining cheese into four small mounds on the skillet, spaced well apart, and heat until melted. Using a spatula, transfer the chips to a plate to cool and harden. Make the chips in two batches if your skillet is not big enough to space them out.

3. Place the patties under the preheated broiler and cook for about 4 minutes, until sizzling and turning brown on top. Turn and cook for an additional 4 minutes, until brown and cooked to your liking.

4. Place each burger on a piece of focaccia and drizzle ¼ teaspoon of the oil over each burger. Top with a Parmesan chip and serve immediately.

PARMESAN CHIPS CAN ALSO BE MADE IN THE OVEN ON A NONSTICK BAKING SHEET, OR EVEN IN THE MICROWAVE. JUST MAKE SURE THAT THE CHEESE ISN'T PILED TOO HIGH AND THAT THERE'S PLENTY OF ROOM FOR THE MELTED CHEESE TO SPREAD.

MAHI MAHI BURGER

PREP TIME: 15 minutes, plus cooling and chilling

COOK TIME: 18-20 minutes

PERKED UP WITH BASIL AND FRESH PARMESAN, THESE FISH BURGERS ARE FANTASTICALLY TASTY. THE POLENTA THAT HOLDS ALL THE INGREDIENTS TOGETHER IS VERY EASY TO PREPARE.

MAKES 4—6

1¼ cups water

1¼ cups instant polenta

1 pound mahi mahi, pollack, or tilapia fillets, skinned

1 tablespoon chopped fresh basil

⅔ cup freshly grated Parmesan cheese

2 tablespoons all-purpose flour

1-2 tablespoons olive oil

salt and pepper

Aioli (see page 192)

4-6 wedges of ciabatta bread

baby spinach leaves and roasted Mediterranean vegetables, to serve

1. Place the water in a large saucepan and bring to a boil. Slowly pour in the polenta in a steady stream and cook over gentle heat, stirring continuously, for 5 minutes, or according to the package directions, until thick. Let cool for about 10 minutes.

2. Place the polenta, fish, basil, and cheese in a food processor or blender, season with salt and pepper, and, using the pulse button, blend together. Shape into four to six equal patties, then coat in the flour. Cover and let chill in the refrigerator for 1 hour.

3. Preheat the grill. Brush the patties with the oil and cook over medium-hot coals for 4-5 minutes on each side, or until cooked through.

4. Place each burger on a ciabatta wedge and top with a spoonful of aioli. Serve immediately with baby spinach leaves and roasted Mediterranean vegetables.

ITALIAN INSTANT POLENTA, A TYPE OF CORNMEAL, IS QUICK TO PREPARE. IT CAN BE FOUND IN SOME SUPERMARKETS. HOWEVER, YOU CAN ALSO USE REGULAR CORNMEAL, FOLLOWING THE PACKAGE DIRECTIONS FOR PREPARING IT.

TURKEY GORGONZOLA BURGER

PREP TIME: 10 minutes   *COOK TIME: 10 minutes*

LEAVE BLAND TURKEY BURGERS BEHIND WITH THESE
BURGERS FILLED WITH BLUE CHEESE AND BLACK PEPPER.
THEY ARE MOIST AND FLAVORSOME ENOUGH
TO STAND ON THEIR OWN.

MAKES 4

2 shallots, finely chopped
½ teaspoon salt
½ teaspoon pepper
⅓ cup crumbled Gorgonzola or other blue cheese
1 pound fresh ground turkey
4 crusty bread rolls, halved

1. Preheat the grill to medium-high. Put the shallots, salt, pepper, and cheese into a bowl and combine. Add the ground turkey and gently break up the meat while working all the ingredients together.

2. Divide the mixture into four equal portions and shape each portion into a patty.

3. Place the patties on the grill and cook for about 4 minutes on each side, until brown and cooked through. Place the burgers in the rolls and serve immediately.

PORCINI BURGER

PREP TIME: 10 minutes   **COOK TIME:** less than 10 minutes

DRIED PORCINI, A TYPE OF MUSHROOM, GROUND TO A POWDER DELICATELY PERFUME AND SEASON THE BEEF IN THESE BURGERS.

MAKES 4

2 ounces dried porcini mushrooms

2 tablespoons olive oil, plus extra for greasing

1 teaspoon salt

½ teaspoon pepper

1 pound fresh ground beef

½ cup shredded Swiss or Gruyère cheese

4 brioche buns, halved

4 teaspoons softened butter

Caramelized Onions (see page 202)

1. Grind the mushrooms to a powder in a spice grinder or clean coffee grinder. You should have about 2 tablespoons. Put the powder into a bowl with the oil, salt, and pepper and stir until the salt is dissolved. If necessary, add up to 2 teaspoons of water to thin the mixture. Add the ground beef and gently mix to combine, then divide into four equal portions and form each portion into a patty.

2. Heat a ridged grill pan or skillet over medium-high heat, then coat with oil. Put the patties in the pan and cover. Cook for about 4 minutes on each side, until browned. After 2 minutes, put the cheese on top of the burgers and cook for an additional 2 minutes, until the burgers are browned and cooked to your liking.

3. Spread the buns with butter and place the burgers in the buns. Top with the onions and serve immediately.

STEP 1

STEP 2

WILD MUSHROOMS HAVE A MUCH EARTHIER FLAVOR THAN CULTIVATED ONES AND A MUCH STRONGER TASTE. PORCINI ARE ESPECIALLY DELICIOUS, BUT CAN BE EXPENSIVE. PORTOBELLO OR CAESAR'S MUSHROOMS, IF YOU CAN FIND THEM, WOULD ALSO BE A GOOD CHOICE.

SMOKED SALT BURGER

PREP TIME: *30 minutes*   **COOK TIME:** *20 minutes*

FLAVORED SALTS ARE A GREAT WAY TO ADD QUICK AND EASY FLAVOR TO BURGERS. HERE, SMOKED SALT ADDS A LIGHTLY SMOKED FLAVOR TO OPEN-FACED BURGERS TOPPED WITH BRIGHT CHARGRILLED SUMMER VEGETABLES.

MAKES 6

2 small zucchini

2 tomatoes

6 thick sourdough bread slices

2 tablespoons olive oil, plus 1 tablespoon for drizzling

1½ pounds fresh ground beef

1½ teaspoons smoked salt, plus extra to taste

1. Preheat the broiled to high. Cut the ends and two sides off the zucchini, then cut lengthwise into ½-inch strips. You will need a total of 12 long, thin strips.

2. Cut the tops and bottoms off the tomatoes, then thickly slice widthwise.

3. Brush the zucchini, tomatoes, and bread with the oil.

4. Combine the ground beef and the smoked salt in a bowl. Divide into six equal portions and shape each portion into a patty.

5. Put the vegetables and bread on the rack. Cook for about 3 minutes on each side, until rack marks appear and the zucchini are tender. Remove from the heat and season with smoked salt.

6. Put the patties on the rack and cook for 4 minutes on each side, or until cooked to your liking. Place each burger on a piece of the chargrilled bread and season with smoked salt. Top each burger with two zucchini slices and one to two tomato slices. Drizzle with oil and serve immediately.

SMOKED SALT CAN BE BOUGHT IN ALL GOOD SUPERMARKETS, BUT IT'S ALSO SURPRISINGLY EASY TO MAKE YOUR OWN. THERE ARE BARBECUE, STOVE-TOP, BROILER, AND EVEN WOK METHODS.

BLUE CHEESE-STUFFED BURGER

PREP TIME: 20 minutes   *COOK TIME: 10 minutes*

INSTEAD OF RAW ONIONS, THESE OOZING-WITH-CHEESE BURGERS ARE ALSO DELICIOUS TOPPED WITH A SWEET-AND-SOUR FIG RELISH (SEE PAGE 94).

MAKES 4

1¼ pounds fresh ground beef
1 teaspoon salt
½ teaspoon pepper
2-3 ounces blue cheese, cut into 4 chunks
vegetable oil, for frying
4 brioche buns, halved
lettuce leaves
tomato slices
red onion slices

1. Put the ground beef into a medium bowl with the salt and pepper and gently mix to combine. Divide into four equal portions and roll each portion into a ball. Use your finger to make a hole in each ball, then stuff a chunk of cheese inside. Press to seal the outside and flatten into ½-inch thick patties.

2. Place a large, nonstick skillet or ridged grill pan over medium-high heat. Add enough vegetable oil to just cover the bottom, then add the patties and cook for 4-5 minutes on each side, until brown and cooked through (some cheese may escape).

3. Put the burgers in the buns, top with the lettuce leaves, tomato, and onion, and serve immediately.

STEP 1

STEP 2

STEP 3

THIS IS A PARTICULARLY IMPRESSIVE BURGER—AND CERTAINLY ONE FOR BLUE CHEESE LOVERS. MAKE THIS RECIPE TO IMPRESS YOUR GUESTS AT A SUMMER BARBECUE, OR EVEN A DINNER PARTY.

FOUR-PEPPER VEAL BURGER

PREP TIME: *25 minutes*   **COOK TIME:** *20 minutes*

THESE BURGERS HIGHLIGHT THE TENDER TEXTURE OF
GROUND VEAL WITH A HIT OF FOUR-COLOR PEPPERCORNS.
LIGHTLY FRIED SHALLOTS AND PEPPERY ARUGULA
MAKE THESE BURGERS SPECIAL.

MAKES 4

3 shallots
2 tablespoons olive oil
1 pound fresh ground veal
1 teaspoon salt
½ teaspoon mixed ground black, white, green, and pink peppercorns
4 pieces of focaccia, 6 x 6 inches and halved
large handful of arugula leaves

1. Peel and thinly slice the shallots, then separate the rings. Heat the oil in a large skillet over high heat until shimmering and add the shallot rings. They should sizzle immediately. Cook for about 10 minutes, stirring occasionally, until well browned. Use a slotted spoon or tongs to remove the shallots from the oil and drain on layers of paper towels. Set the skillet aside.

2. Put the ground veal into a large bowl and sprinkle with the salt and peppercorns. Gently break up the meat and toss with the seasoning until well combined. Divide into four equal portions and shape each portion into a patty.

3. Pour most of the oil out of the skillet and return the skillet to the stove. Heat to medium-high heat, add the patties, and cook for about 4 minutes on each side, until brown and cooked to your liking.

4. Place each burger on a piece of focaccia and top with the fried shallots, arugula, and the remaining pieces of focaccia. Serve immediately.

STEP 3

STEP 1

GROUND VEAL CAN SOMETIMES BE DIFFICULT TO FIND IN THE SUPERMARKET. IF THIS IS THE CASE, YOU CAN SUBSTITUTE WITH CHICKEN, TURKEY, OR EVEN LAMB.

113

PORTOBELLO MUSHROOM BURGER WITH MOZZARELLA

PREP TIME: *10 minutes* **COOK TIME:** *15 minutes*

THIS VEGETARIAN BURGER COMBINES MARINATED PORTOBELLO MUSHROOMS WITH MOZZARELLA CHEESE AND PESTO IN A FOCACCIA "BUN."

MAKES 4

4 teaspoons olive oil

2 teaspoons red wine vinegar

1 garlic clove, finely chopped

4 large portobello mushrooms, caps only

fresh vegetarian mozzarella-style cheese slices

4 pieces focaccia, 6 x 6 inches and halved

¼ cup pesto

tomato slices

baby arugula leaves

salt and pepper

1. Preheat the broiler to high and the oven to 325°F. Whisk together the oil, vinegar, and garlic in a medium bowl. Place the mushrooms, gill side up, on a baking sheet, then drizzle with the vinaigrette and season with salt and pepper.

2. Place under the preheated broiler and cook for about 5-8 minutes, until the mushrooms are tender. Place the cheese slices on top and cook for an additional 1-2 minutes, until bubbling. Meanwhile, put the focaccia on the lower rack in the preheated oven for 5 minutes to warm through.

3. Lightly spread the focaccia with the pesto, then add the mushrooms. Top with the tomato slices and arugula and serve immediately.

THIS IS A PERFECT BURGER TO SERVE TO VEGETARIAN GUESTS—JUST MAKE SURE THAT ANY CHEESE USED IS SUITABLE FOR VEGETARIANS, TOO. IT SHOULDN'T CONTAIN ANY ANIMAL RENNET.

SLIDERS

PREP TIME: *15 minutes*   **COOK TIME:** *7 minutes*

SLIDERS ARE MINI BURGERS THAT MAY HAVE BEEN NAMED FOR THE WAY THEY SLID AROUND WHEN SERVED IN THE GALLEYS OF TOSSING AND TURNING U.S. NAVY SHIPS AT SEA.

MAKES 12

1 pound fresh ground beef

1 teaspoon salt

½ teaspoon pepper

1–2 teaspoons butter

3 ounces American or cheddar cheese slices, cut into 2-inch squares

12 mini hamburger buns or slider buns, halved

1. Place the ground beef in a medium bowl, add the salt and pepper, then divide into 12 equal portions and shape each portion into a patty.

2. Heat a ridged grill pan over medium-high heat. Add enough butter to lightly coat the pan, using a spatula to spread it over the bottom. Add the patties and cook for 3 minutes on one side, until brown, then turn and add the cheese. Cook for an additional 2-3 minutes, or until brown and cooked to your liking.

3. Place the burgers in the buns and serve immediately.

KA-BOOM!!

STEP 1

STEP 2

STEP 2

THESE SMALL BURGERS ARE PERFECT FOR ENTERTAINING. FOR LARGE CROWDS, MAKE THE PATTIES WITH DIFFERENT MEATS TO PROVIDE YOUR GUESTS WITH A VARIATION OF TASTES AND TEXTURES.

JAMAICAN JERK CHICKEN BURGER

PREP TIME: *25 minutes*   **COOK TIME:** *20 minutes*

GROUND CHICKEN IS SPICED UP WITH JAMAICAN JERK SEASONING FOR THESE DELICIOUS BURGERS.

MAKES 4

1 teaspoon light brown sugar

1 teaspoon ground ginger

½ teaspoon ground allspice

½ teaspoon dried thyme

½–1 teaspoon cayenne pepper

1 tablespoon lime juice

2 garlic cloves, minced

½ teaspoon salt

½ teaspoon pepper

1 pound fresh ground chicken

1 tablespoon vegetable oil

1 red or yellow bell pepper, seeded and cut into large flat pieces

1 teaspoon olive oil

1 teaspoon red wine vinegar

4 onion hamburger buns, halved

lettuce leaves

salt and pepper

1. Place the sugar, ginger, allspice, thyme, cayenne pepper, lime juice, garlic, salt, and pepper into a bowl and mix together. Add the chicken and gently mix to combine. Divide the mixture into four equal portions and shape each portion into a patty.

2. Place a ridged grill pan over medium–high heat and add the vegetable oil. Add the bell pepper and cook for about 5 minutes, turning frequently, until blackened. Transfer to a bowl, cover with plastic wrap or a plate, and let steam for 5 minutes. Remove the skin and cut the flesh into strips. Toss with the olive oil, and vinegar, and season with salt and pepper.

3. Put the patties in the pan and cook, covered, for about 5 minutes on each side, until brown and cooked through. Place the burgers in the buns and top with the lettuce and bell peppers. Serve immediately.

STEP 1

STEP 3

To spice up these burgers even more, serve with homemade pickled jalapeños on the side (see page 198).

THE LONDON BURGER

FEEL FREE TO COOK THE EGGS TO YOUR LIKING, BUT NOTE THAT HAVING SOME RUNNY YOLK MAKES A WONDERFUL SAUCE ON THESE BURGERS.

MAKES 4

1 pound fresh ground beef

2 tablespoons Worcestershire sauce

4 English muffins

4 tablespoons butter

2 teaspoons vegetable oil

4 eggs

1/2 teaspoon salt

1/2 teaspoon pepper

1. Combine the ground beef with half the Worcestershire sauce in a large bowl. Divide the mixture into four equal portions and shape each portion into a patty about 1/2 inch wider than the muffins, making a dimple in the center of each patty.

2. Halve the muffins and spread each half with butter.

3. Heat a large skillet over medium-high heat. Place the muffin halves in the skillet, buttered side down, and cook for about 2 minutes. Put two muffin halves on each of four plates.

4. Add the patties to the skillet and cook for about 4 minutes, until brown. Turn and cook on the other side for 4 minutes, until brown and cooked to your liking. Place a burger on one of the muffin halves on each plate and drizzle with the remaining Worcestershire sauce.

5. Add the oil to the skillet, swirling to coat. Add the eggs and sprinkle with the salt and pepper. Cover and cook for about 3 minutes, until the whites are set and the yolks are beginning to set at the edges. Top each burger with an egg and the top half of a muffin. Serve immediately.

THESE BURGERS WOULD MAKE THE PERFECT BREAKFAST TREAT. WHY NOT ADD SOME CRISPY BACON AND HOMEMADE KETCHUP (SEE PAGE 170) FOR ADDED INDULGENCE.

MOROCCAN LAMB BURGER

PREP TIME: *20 minutes, plus standing*   **COOK TIME:** *12 minutes*

MAKES 4

1¼ pounds fresh ground lamb

1 onion, grated

1 teaspoon harissa sauce

1 garlic clove, crushed

2 tablespoons finely chopped fresh mint

½ teaspoon cumin seeds, crushed

½ teaspoon paprika

oil, for greasing

salt and pepper

4 pita breads, warmed

red onion slices

shredded lettuce leaves

YOGURT & CUCUMBER SAUCE

½ large cucumber

¼ cup plain yogurt

⅓ cup chopped fresh mint

salt

1. To make the sauce, peel the cucumber, quarter it lengthwise, and scoop out the seeds. Chop the flesh and put in a strainer set over a bowl. Sprinkle with salt, cover with a plate, and weigh down with a can of vegetables. Let drain for 30 minutes, then mix with the remaining ingredients.

2. Combine the lamb, onion, harissa sauce, garlic, mint, cumin seeds, and paprika. Season with salt and pepper, mixing well with a fork. Divide into four equal portions and flatten into patties about 1 inch thick. Cover and let stand at room temperature for 30 minutes.

3. Preheat the grill. Lightly brush the patties with oil. Grease the grill grate. Cook over hot coals for 5-6 minutes on each side, or until cooked through.

4. Stuff the burgers into warm pita breads with the red onion, lettuce leaves, and a spoonful of the sauce. Serve immediately.

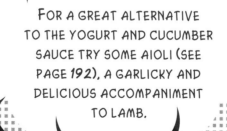

FOR A GREAT ALTERNATIVE TO THE YOGURT AND CUCUMBER SAUCE TRY SOME AIOLI (SEE PAGE *192*), A GARLICKY AND DELICIOUS ACCOMPANIMENT TO LAMB.

THE AUSSIE BURGER

PREP TIME: 20 minutes   **COOK TIME: less than 12 minutes**

AUSTRALIANS LOVE TO PUT BEET ON THEIR BURGERS. GRILLED PINEAPPLE AND FRIED EGGS ARE OTHER AUSSIE ADD-ONS THAT MAKE THIS MILE-HIGH BURGER EXTRA SATISFYING.

MAKES 4

1 pound fresh ground beef

1 teaspoon salt

½ teaspoon pepper

4 canned pineapple slices

2-3 teaspoons vegetable oil, for brushing and frying

4 eggs

mayonnaise, for spreading

4 soft hamburger buns, halved

4-8 beet slices in vinegar

lettuce leaves

tomato slices

salt and pepper

1. Place the ground beef in a medium bowl with 1 teaspoon of salt and ½ teaspoon of pepper. Mix gently to combine, then divide into four equal portions and shape each portion into a patty.

2. Place a ridged grill pan over medium-high heat and add 1 teaspoon of the oil. Lightly brush the pineapple with oil and place the patties and pineapple in the pan. Cover and cook the pineapple for 3 minutes on each side, until it is soft and marked, and cook the burgers for about 4 minutes on each side, until brown and cooked to your liking. Remove from the heat and keep warm.

3. Add enough oil to a skillet to lightly cover the bottom, swirling to coat the skillet. Add the eggs and season with salt and pepper. Cover and cook for about 3 minutes, until the whites are set and the yolks are beginning to set at the edges.

4. Spread some mayonnaise on each half of the buns. Place a pineapple slice on each bun bottom, then add a burger, egg, one to two beet slices, a lettuce leaf, and a tomato slice. Finish with the bun tops and serve immediately.

STEP 2

STEP 3

STEP 4

OTHER TRADITIONAL
ACCOMPANIMENTS TO THIS
MONUMENTAL BURGER INCLUDE
BACON AND CHEESE. ALL YOU
NEED TO DO NEXT IS WORK OUT
HOW TO ATTACK IT!

BARBECUED CAJUN PORK BURGER

PREP TIME: *20 minutes, plus chilling*   **COOK TIME:** *35–45 minutes*

MAKES 4–6

1 large sweet potato (about 8 ounces), cut into chunks

1 pound fresh ground pork

1 apple, such as McIntosh, peeled, cored, and grated

2 teaspoons Cajun seasoning

4 onions

1 tablespoon chopped fresh cilantro

2 tablespoons sunflower oil

8–12 bacon strips

salt and pepper

1. Cook the sweet potato in a saucepan of lightly salted, boiling water for 15-20 minutes, or until soft when pierced with a fork. Drain well, then mash and reserve.

2. Place the pork in a bowl, add the mashed sweet potato, apple, and Cajun seasoning. Grate one of the onions and add to the pork mixture with the cilantro and season with salt and pepper. Mix together, then shape into four to six equal patties. Cover and let chill in the refrigerator for 1 hour.

3. Slice the remaining onions. Heat 1 tablespoon of the oil in a skillet. Add the onions and cook over low heat for 10-12 minutes, stirring until soft. Remove the skillet from the heat and reserve. Wrap each patty in two bacon strips.

4. Preheat the grill. Cook the patties over hot coals, brushing with the remaining oil, for 4-5 minutes on each side, or until thoroughly cooked. Alternatively, cook in a ridged grill pan or under a hot broiler. Serve immediately with the fried onions.

THE CAJUN SEASONING REALLY LIVENS UP THE FLAVOR OF THESE PORK BURGERS. YOU SHOULD KEEP THIS SEASONING IN A COOL, DARK PLACE. IF EXPOSED TO HEAT OR LIGHT, ITS PUNGENCY QUICKLY DISAPPEARS.

THAI CRAB BURGER

PREP TIME: *10 minutes, plus chilling*   **COOK TIME:** *10 minutes*

MAKES 4

1½ tablespoons sunflower oil

1 fresh red chile, seeded and finely chopped

1-inch piece fresh ginger, grated

2 lemongrass stalks, outer leaves removed and finely chopped

2 (6-ounce) cans white crabmeat, drained and flaked

8 ounces cooked, peeled shrimp, thawed if frozen and squeezed dry

1 cup cooked jasmine rice

1 tablespoon chopped fresh cilantro

1 cup bean sprouts

6 scallions, finely chopped

1 tablespoon soy sauce

1-2 tablespoons whole-wheat flour

1. Heat a wok or skillet. When hot, add 2 teaspoons of the oil, the chile, ginger, and lemongrass and stir-fry over medium-high heat for 1 minute. Remove the wok from the heat and let cool.

2. Place the chile mixture, crabmeat, shrimp, rice, chopped cilantro, bean sprouts, scallions, and soy sauce in a food processor or blender and, using the pulse button, blend together. Shape into four equal patties, then coat in the flour. Cover and let chill in the refrigerator for 1 hour.

3. Heat a heavy, nonstick skillet and add the remaining oil. When hot, add the patties and cook over medium heat for 3-4 minutes on each side, or until piping hot. Serve immediately.

STEP 1

STEP 2

STEP 2

CRABMEAT IS A GREAT
SOURCE OF PROTEIN AND IS
ALSO LOW IN FAT AND HAS FEW
CALORIES. SERVE THIS DELICIOUS
BURGER WITH TARTAR SAUCE
(SEE PAGE 182).

HAWAIIAN BURGER

PREP TIME: 25 minutes   **COOK TIME: 10 minutes**

THE FLAVORS OF THE HAWAIIAN ISLANDS COME INTO PLAY IN THIS PORK BURGER SERVED WITH CHARGRILLED PINEAPPLE.

MAKES 4

1 pound fresh ground pork

3 tablespoons teriyaki sauce, plus extra for spreading

4 canned pineapple slices

onion slices

vegetable oil, for brushing

4 Hawaiian buns, or soft white hamburger buns, halved

lettuce leaves

1. Preheat the grill to medium-high. Put the ground pork into a medium bowl and season with the teriyaki sauce, mixing gently until incorporated. Divide into four equal portions and form each portion into a patty.

2. Lightly brush the pineapple and onion with oil. Place the patties, onion, and pineapple on the grill and cover. Cook the onion and pineapple for 3-4 minutes on each side, until soft and marked. Cook the burgers for 4 minutes on each side, until brown and cooked through.

3. Spread both halves of the buns with teriyaki sauce. Put the burgers in the buns with the pineapple, onion, and lettuce and serve immediately.

STEP 1

STEP 2

JAPANESE IMMIGRANTS TO HAWAII HELPED MAKE INGREDIENTS SUCH AS TERIYAKI SAUCE AN INTEGRAL PART OF THE LOCAL DIET. IN FACT, WHAT'S CALLED HAWAIIAN BARBECUE SAUCE IS BASICALLY TERIYAKI SAUCE.

MEXICAN TURKEY BURGER

PREP TIME: 10 minutes, plus chilling   **COOK TIME: 10-12 minutes**

MAKES 4

1 pound fresh ground turkey

¾ cup of canned refried beans

2-4 garlic cloves, crushed

1-2 fresh jalapeño chiles, seeded and finely chopped

2 tablespoons tomato paste

1 tablespoon chopped fresh cilantro

1 tablespoon sunflower oil

salt and pepper

shredded baby spinach leaves

4 cheese-topped hamburger buns, halved

salsa

Guacamole (see page 186)

tortilla chips, to serve

1. Place the ground turkey in a bowl and break up any large lumps. Beat the refried beans until smooth, then add to the turkey in the bowl.

2. Add the garlic, chiles, tomato paste, and cilantro, season with salt and pepper, and mix together. Shape into four equal patties, then cover and let chill in the refrigerator for 1 hour.

3. Preheat the grill. Brush the patties with the oil and cook over medium-hot coals for 5-6 minutes on each side, or until cooked through.

4. Place the spinach on the bottom halves of the hamburger buns and top with the burgers. Spoon over a little salsa and guacamole and top with the lids. Serve immediately with tortilla chips on the side.

WHAM!

There are many varieties of fresh chiles available. If you are in doubt about how much of the chile's heat you prefer, start with the milder chiles, such as jalapeño, and gradually move on to the hotter ones.

ARGENTINE BURGER WITH CHIMICHURRI

PREP TIME: 25 minutes, plus chilling

COOK TIME: less than 15 minutes

USING FRESH GROUND BEEF ADDS AN EXTRA BEEFY FLAVOR TO THESE BURGERS INSPIRED BY THE BARBECUED STEAKS AND TANGY CHIMICHURRI SAUCE OF ARGENTINA.

MAKES 4

1 pound boneless chuck roast, round, or boneless short ribs, or a mixture with at least 20 percent fat

¼ cup finely chopped onion

2 tablespoons fresh lemon juice

2 tablespoons finely chopped fresh parsley

2 tablespoons finely chopped fresh mint

1 garlic clove, minced

1 teaspoon crushed red pepper (optional)

¼ cup olive oil

4 French rolls, halved

avocado slices

salt and pepper

1. Preheat the grill to medium-high. Cut the beef into 1-inch cubes, then place on a plate, wrap in plastic wrap, and chill in the refrigerator for about 30 minutes, until cold.

2. Meanwhile, put the onion, lemon juice, parsley, mint, garlic, and crushed red pepper, if using, into a small bowl, season with salt and pepper, and combine. Stir in the oil and set aside.

3. Place half the beef in a food processor or blender and pulse about 15 times. Season with salt and pepper and pulse an additional 10-15 times until the meat is finely chopped but not overprocessed. Remove from the processor and repeat with the remaining meat.

4. Divide the meat into four equal portions and shape each portion into a patty.

5. Place the patties on the grill and cook for 3 minutes on each side for medium-rare, and 4 minutes on each side for medium.

6. Place the burgers in the rolls. Top with the avocado slices and a few spoonfuls of the sauce. Serve immediately.

STEP 2

STEP 3

STEP 6

CHIMICHURRI IS TRADITIONALLY
SERVED WITH STEAK, HENCE THE
BRAISING STEAK USED IN THIS
RECIPE. IT IS ALSO DELICIOUS
SERVED WITH CHICKEN OR FISH.

BENTO BURGER

PREP TIME: *15 minutes, plus resting*   **COOK TIME:** *15 minutes*

THESE JAPANESE VEGAN SNACKS ARE MADE WITH COOKED RICE PRESSED INTO THE SHAPE OF BUNS, CRISP ON THE OUTSIDE, WITH SAVORY SPINACH INSIDE.

MAKES 5

8 shiitake mushrooms, stems removed

1 pound washed spinach leaves

2 tablespoons soy sauce

2 tablespoons mirin

2 teaspoons sesame seeds, toasted

1 teaspoon salt

1 cup lukewarm water

2 cups short- or medium-grain white rice, rinsed, cooked, and kept warm

2 teaspoons sesame oil, for frying

1. Preheat the broiler to high. Arrange the mushrooms on the broiler pan and cook for 3 minutes on each side, until brown and tender. Thinly slice the mushrooms and place in a medium bowl.

2. Bring a large saucepan of water to a boil. Add the spinach and blanch for 1 minute. Drain, cool under cold running water, then squeeze dry. Add the mushrooms to the spinach, then add the soy sauce, mirin, and sesame seeds and combine.

3. Dissolve the salt in the warm water. Place the rice in a wide bowl and divide into 10 equal portions. Wet your hands with the water and firmly press each portion into a bun shape. Wet your hands each time you make a bun. Let set for 20 minutes.

4. Place a nonstick skillet or ridged grill pan over medium heat and lightly coat the bottom with oil. Add the rice buns and cook for 4 minutes on each side (turning gently), until brown.

5. Put the spinach mixture on top of half the rice buns, then top with the remaining buns. Wrap the burgers in squares of parchment paper to hold them together prior to serving and serve within 2 hours.

STEP 3

STEP 1

RINSING THE RICE HELPS IT STICK TOGETHER, AND USING SHORT- OR MEDIUM-GRAIN RICE IS ESSENTIAL.

KIMCHI BURGER

PREP TIME: *20 minutes*   **COOK TIME:** *20 minutes*

THE BRIGHT, SPICY TASTE OF KOREAN KIMCHI
(SPICY FERMENTED CABBAGE) IS HIGHLIGHTED
WITH SAUTÉED SCALLIONS AND GINGER
IN THESE JUICY BURGERS.

MAKES 6

1 pound fresh
ground beef

8 ounces fresh
ground pork

1 tablespoon finely
grated fresh ginger

1 teaspoon soy sauce

10 scallions

1 teaspoon vegetable oil

6 sesame seed
hamburger buns, halved

1 cup kimchi

1. Preheat the grill to high. Put the beef, pork, ginger, and soy sauce into a large bowl and mix to combine. Finely chop two scallions and mix them into the meat. Divide the mixture into six equal portions and shape each portion into a patty. Cover and chill in the refrigerator.

2. Meanwhile, cut the remaining scallions into 4-inch lengths and brush them with oil. Place on the grill and cook for about 5 minutes, turning, until tender and brown. Set aside.

3. Place the patties on the grill and cook for about 4 minutes on each side, until they are marked and cooked through.

4. Put the burgers in the buns and top with the scallions and some kimchi. Serve immediately.

KA-POW!

YOU CAN BUY KIMCHI FROM ASIAN GROCERY STORES, OR EVEN MAKE YOUR OWN AT HOME. THERE ARE MANY VARIATIONS, SO YOU CAN DECIDE UPON THE RECIPE THAT BEST SUITS YOUR TASTES OR MOOD.

GREEN CHILE CHEESE BURGER

PREP TIME: *25 minutes*   **COOK TIME:** *20 minutes*

IT'S EASY ENOUGH TO THROW SOME ROASTED GREEN CHILES AND SOME CHEESE ON A BURGER, BUT THIS RECIPE WORKS THOSE FLAVORS INTO THE MEAT FOR A SUPREMELY MOIST BURGER WITH A SOUTHWESTERN FLAIR.

MAKES 6

3 large, mild green chiles

1½ pounds fresh ground beef

1 teaspoon salt

1 cup grated Monterey Jack or cheddar cheese, grated, plus 6 slices

6 soft hamburger buns, halved

1. Preheat the grill to high. Place the chiles on the rack and cook, turning frequently, until black all over. Wrap them in aluminum foil and let stand for 15 minutes. Peel off the skins, remove the stems, and finely chop.

2. Put the ground beef, salt, chopped chiles, and grated cheese into a large bowl and gently mix to combine.

3. Divide the mixture into six equal portions and form each portion into a patty. Place the patties on the grill and cook for 4 minutes. Turn, top each burger with a slice of cheese, then cover and cook for an additional 4 minutes, until cooked to your liking and the cheese is melted. Place the burgers in the buns and serve immediately.

STEP 1

STEP 2

STEP 3

THIS RECIPE USES LARGE MILD CHILES, BUT IF YOU PREFER A HOTTER BURGER, JUST REPLACE WITH SOME FIERY FRESH THAI CHILES INSTEAD.

LAMB-CUMIN PITA BURGER WITH TAHINI SAUCE

PREP TIME: 25 minutes

COOK TIME: less than 15 minutes

THESE PITA BURGERS ARE A LITTLE SMALLER THAN THE AVERAGE BURGER, BUT THE RICH LAMB PATTIES TOPPED WITH FRESH VEGETABLES AND TAHINI SAUCE ARE FILLING.

MAKES 6

1 pound fresh ground lamb

3 tablespoons finely chopped red onion

1 tablespoon chopped fresh cilantro, plus extra leaves to garnish

1 teaspoon salt

½ teaspoon pepper

½ teaspoon ground cumin

⅓ cup tahini

⅓ plain yogurt

1 garlic clove, minced

3 large pita breads, warmed and halved

tomato slices

cucumber slices

olive oil, for drizzling

salt and pepper

1. Preheat the broiler to high and line the broiler pan with aluminum foil. Place the lamb in a medium bowl, and add the onion, cilantro, 1 teaspoon of salt, ½ teaspoon of pepper, and the cumin, then gently mix to combine. Divide into six equal portions, form each portion into a 3-inch wide patty, and place in the prepared broiler pan.

2. Place the pan under the preheated broiler and cook the patties for about 5-7 minutes on each side, or until cooked through and brown.

3. Put the tahini, yogurt, and garlic into a bowl, season with salt and pepper, and mix to combine. Stuff the burgers into the pita halves, then drizzle the tahini sauce over them. Add the tomato and cucumber slices and the cilantro leaves, drizzle with the oil, and serve immediately.

TAHINI, OR SESAME SEED PASTE, MAKES A VERSATILE ADDITION TO THE KITCHEN CABINET. THE DARKER VERSION IS PREFERABLE BECAUSE IT DOESN'T HAVE THE NUTRITIOUS OUTER HULL REMOVED, BUT IT CAN BE A LITTLE RICH FOR SOME TASTES.

KHEEMA BURGER WITH RAITA

PREP TIME: 30 minutes   **COOK TIME:** 15 minutes

LIKE AN INDIAN RAITA, YOGURT SAUCE AND WILTED CUCUMBERS COOL OFF THE SPICE IN THESE DELICIOUS BURGERS.

MAKES 6

2 tablespoons vegetable oil

1 onion, chopped

1 pound fresh ground beef

2-inch piece fresh ginger, finely chopped

2 garlic cloves, minced

1 teaspoon ground coriander

1 teaspoon ground cumin

1 teaspoon salt

½ teaspoon turmeric

½ teaspoon cayenne pepper

½ teaspoon ground nutmeg

6 thin flatbreads

YOGURT SAUCE

1 small garlic clove, minced

½ teaspoon garam masala

½ teaspoon salt

1 teaspoon lemon juice

1 cup Greek-style yogurt

CUCUMBER RELISH

1 small cucumber

½ teaspoon salt

2 teaspoons lemon juice

1. Add 1 tablespoon of the oil to a large skillet over high heat. Add the onion and cook for about 10 minutes, stirring frequently, until beginning to brown. Remove from the skillet and set aside, leaving any remaining oil in the skillet.

2. Meanwhile, to make the sauce, stir the garlic, garam masala, salt, and lemon juice into the yogurt. Set aside to develop the flavors. To prepare the cucumber relish, halve lengthwise, seed, and finely chop the cucumber, then toss with the salt and lemon juice. Set aside to develop the flavors.

3. Put the ground beef into a large bowl with the onion, ginger, garlic, coriander, cumin, salt, turmeric, cayenne pepper, and nutmeg and mix to combine. Divide into six equal portions and shape each portion into a 6-inch-long oval patty.

4. Return the skillet to high heat and add the remaining oil. Add the patties and cook on one side for about 5 minutes, until brown. Turn and cook on the other side for about 5 minutes, or until cooked to your liking.

5. Set each burger on a piece of flatbread, top with 1 tablespoon of the yogurt sauce, and a portion of the cucumber relish. Roll the sides of the flatbread to encase the filling. Serve immediately with any remaining yogurt sauce and cucumber relish.

STEP 5

STEP 1

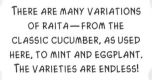
THERE ARE MANY VARIATIONS OF RAITA—FROM THE CLASSIC CUCUMBER, AS USED HERE, TO MINT AND EGGPLANT. THE VARIETIES ARE ENDLESS!

SPICED LENTIL-POTATO BURGER

PREP TIME: *30 minutes*   **COOK TIME:** *45 minutes*

WHOLESOME AND VEGETARIAN, THESE BURGER PATTIES ARE
MADE WITH LENTILS SIMMERED IN INDIAN SPICES
AND BOUND WITH MASHED POTATO.

MAKES 6

½ cup green lentils

1 carrot, peeled and diced

2 tablespoons vegetable oil, plus extra for frying

1 tablespoon brown mustard seeds

1 teaspoon ground coriander

1 teaspoon ground cumin

½ onion, finely chopped

1 teaspoon minced garlic

1 fresh serrano chile, finely chopped, or ½ teaspoon cayenne pepper

⅓ cup frozen peas, thawed

1 potato, cooked, peeled, and mashed

1¼ cups fresh bread crumbs

6 whole-wheat hamburger buns, halved

store-bought cilantro chutney or mango chutney

lettuce leaves

salt and pepper

1. Bring a large saucepan of lightly salted water to a boil. Add the lentils, bring back to a boil, then reduce the heat and simmer for 15 minutes. Add the carrot and cook for about 10 minutes, until the lentils are soft. Drain.

2. Heat the oil in a medium sauté pan. Add the mustard seeds, coriander, and cumin and swirl to coat in the oil. Add the onion, garlic, and chile and cook for 5-8 minutes, stirring frequently, until the onion is soft. Stir in the lentils and carrot and simmer for about 5 minutes to evaporate any liquid. Add the peas and potato and season with salt and pepper, then combine thoroughly.

3. Place the bread crumbs in a shallow bowl. Scoop out the lentil mixture in six equal portions and shape each portion into a patty. Press each patty in the bread crumbs to cover both sides.

4. Place a ridged grill pan or large skillet over medium heat and add enough oil to coat the bottom. Add the patties and cook for about 5 minutes on each side until brown.

5. Place the burgers in the buns, top with the chutney and lettuce leaves, and serve immediately.

WITH **26** PERCENT OF THEIR CALORIFIC VALUE COMING FROM PROTEIN, LENTILS ARE AN IMPORTANT STAPLE IN ANY DIET, CREATING STRONG SKIN, NAILS, AND HAIR.

SHRIMP CHIVE BURGER WITH CHOW CHOW

PREP TIME: *20 minutes,*
plus chilling   COOK TIME: *10 minutes*

THIS RECIPE COULDN'T BE SIMPLER—OR TASTIER. GENTLY COOKING THE SHRIMP OVER MEDIUM HEAT HELPS KEEP THEM MOIST AND TENDER ... AND UTTERLY DELICIOUS.

MAKES 4

1 pound shrimp, peeled and deveined

1 bunch chives or 2 scallions

1 teaspoon vegetable oil

4 brioche buns or soft hamburger buns, halved

1 cup Chow Chow (Corn Relish, see page 190)

1. Coarsely chop the shrimp, then place half in a food processor or blender and process until pastelike, or finely chop with a knife. Stir together the paste and chopped shrimp. Snip the chives and stir them into the shrimp.

2. Divide the shrimp mixture into four equal portions. Using damp hands, shape each portion into a patty. Transfer the patties to a plate, cover, and chill in the refrigerator for at least 30 minutes or overnight.

3. Heat the oil in a large, nonstick skillet over medium heat and gently place the patties in the skillet. Partly cover the skillet and cook for 6 minutes, until the patties are almost cooked through. Gently turn and cook on the other side for about 1 minute, until pink and cooked through.

4. Place the burgers in the buns and top each with chow chow relish. Serve immediately.

STEP 1

STEP 1

THIS IS TRULY A GOURMET BURGER, AND IT MAKES A GREAT CHANGE OF PACE FROM THE TRADITIONAL BEEF BURGER.

PORK BANH MI BURGER

PREP TIME: *30 minutes, plus marinating*   **COOK TIME:** *10 minutes*

FRAGRANT WITH CHINESE FIVE-SPICE POWDER, THESE BURGERS ARE STUFFED INTO FRENCH ROLLS WITH PICKLED VEGETABLES INSPIRED BY VIETNAMESE BAGUETTE SANDWICHES.

MAKES 4

1 pound fresh ground pork

1 garlic clove, minced

1 tablespoon Thai fish sauce

1 teaspoon Chinese five-spice powder

½ teaspoon sugar

¼ teaspoon pepper

¼ cup mayonnaise

4 French rolls, halved long, thin cucumber strips

handful of fresh cilantro sprigs

1 fresh jalapeño chile, thinly sliced

soy sauce or chili sauce

PICKLED VEGETABLES

3 carrots, cut into julienne strips

½ daikon radish (about 7 ounces), cut into julienne strips

1 teaspoon salt

1 teaspoon sugar

¾ cup distilled vinegar

¾ cup water

1. To make the pickled vegetables, put the carrots and daikon into a medium bowl and toss with the salt and sugar. Add the vinegar and water and let marinate for at least 30 minutes or overnight in the refrigerator.

2. Put the ground pork, garlic, fish sauce, spice powder, sugar, and pepper into a medium bowl and combine. Stir gently, then divide into four equal portions and shape each portion into an oval patty that will fit in a French roll.

3. Place a ridged grill pan over medium-high heat, add the patties, and cook for 5 minutes on each side, until brown and cooked through.

4. Spread mayonnaise on the rolls and stuff each with a burger, cucumber slice, several cilantro sprigs, and and a few chile slices. Drizzle with soy sauce and serve immediately.

STEP 4

STEP 1

WOW YOUR GUESTS WITH THESE AROMATIC AND MOUTHWATERING BURGERS. NOT ONLY ARE THEY DELECTABLE BUT THEY'RE ALSO RATHER BEAUTIFUL TO LOOK AT WITH AN ARRAY OF VIBRANT COLORS.

PEANUT SAUCE CHICKEN BURGER

PREP TIME: 30 minutes   **COOK TIME:** 10 minutes

MAKES 4

1 tablespoon light brown sugar

1 tablespoon soy sauce

1 tablespoon Thai fish sauce

1 tablespoon finely chopped lemongrass

2 teaspoons curry powder

1 garlic clove, minced

½ fresh serrano chile, chopped, or ½ teaspoon cayenne pepper

1 pound fresh ground chicken

peanut oil, for brushing

4 French rolls, halved

pickled onions, thinly sliced

SAUCE

⅓ cup chunky peanut butter

⅓ cup coconut milk

2 tablespoons hot water, plus extra if needed

1 tablespoon Thai fish sauce

1 tablespoon light brown sugar

1 tablespoon soy sauce

2 teaspoons fresh lime juice

1 teaspoon chopped garlic

¼ fresh serrano chile, chopped, or ¼ teaspoon cayenne pepper

1. Put the sugar, soy sauce, fish sauce, lemongrass, curry powder, garlic, and chile into a medium bowl, stir to combine, then mix in the chicken. Divide the mixture into four equal portions, then use damp hands to shape each portion into a ½-inch-thick oval patty.

2. To make the sauce, put all of the ingredients into a food processor or blender and process until smooth. Add more water to loosen, if necessary.

3. Lightly brush a ridged grill pan with oil and heat over medium-high heat. Add the patties and cook for 5 minutes, then turn and cook for an additional 5 minutes, until brown and cooked through.

4. Spread both halves of the rolls with the peanut sauce, then top with the burgers, and some pickled onions. Serve immediately.

STEP 1

STEP 2

STEP 3

THESE BURGERS PUT ALL THE FLAVORS USED TO MARINATE CHICKEN SKEWERS INSIDE JUICY PATTIES, WITH GENEROUS DOLLOPS OF SWEET AND SPICY PEANUT SAUCE ON THE BUNS.

CALIFORNIA TURKEY BURGER

PREP TIME: 15 minutes, plus chilling   **COOK TIME: 10 minutes**

THIS BURGER IS PERFECT FOR WHEN YOU HAVE THAT BURGER CRAVING, BUT WANT TO KEEP THINGS AS HEALTHY (YET DELICIOUS) AS POSSIBLE.

MAKES 4

1 pound fresh ground turkey

1 teaspoon salt

1 avocado

1 tablespoon lemon juice

2 teaspoons olive oil

4 whole-wheat hamburger buns, halved

tomato slices

1 cup bean sprouts

1. Preheat the barbecue to medium. Put the ground turkey into a large bowl and sprinkle with the salt. Gently break up and toss the meat to mix in the salt.

2. Divide the meat into four equal portions and shape each portion into a patty. Chill in the refrigerator for about 15 minutes.

3. Meanwhile, pit, peel, and slice the avocado. Sprinkle the lemon juice over the avocado, toss gently to mix, and set aside.

4. Brush the patties on both sides with oil, then place them on the grill. Cook for about 4 minutes, until they are starting to brown and come away easily from the grill. Turn and cook on the other side for about 4 minutes, until cooked through.

5. Set the burgers on the buns. Top with the avocado slices, tomato slices, and a handful of bean sprouts. Add the bun lids and serve immediately.

BEAN SPROUTS ARE A LOW-CALORIE SOURCE OF MANY NUTRIENTS, INCLUDING VITAMIN C, PROTEIN, CALCIUM, AND FOLATE.

LAMB & FETA BURGER

PREP TIME: *10 minutes, plus chilling*   **COOK TIME:** *10 minutes*

THESE BURGERS ARE ABSOLUTELY DELICIOUS—THE COMBINATION OF THE FETA CHEESE WITH THE PRUNES, PINE NUTS, AND ROSEMARY MAY SOUND SOMEWHAT UNUSUAL, BUT IT TASTES FABULOUS.

MAKES 4-6

1 pound fresh ground lamb

1½ cups crumbled feta cheese

2 garlic cloves, crushed

6 scallions, finely chopped

⅔ cup chopped, pitted prunes

3 tablespoons pine nuts, toasted

1¼ cups fresh whole-wheat bread crumbs

1 tablespoon chopped fresh rosemary

1 tablespoon sunflower oil

salt and pepper

4-6 The Perfect Burger Bun, halved (see page 200)

1. Place the ground lamb in a large bowl with the feta, garlic, scallions, prunes, pine nuts, and bread crumbs. Mix well, breaking up any lumps.

2. Add the rosemary to the lamb mixture and season with salt and pepper. Mix together, then shape into four to six equal patties. Cover and let chill in the refrigerator for 30 minutes.

3. Preheat the grill. Brush the burgers lightly with half the oil and cook over hot coals for 4 minutes, then brush with the remaining oil and turn over. Continue to cook for 4 minutes, or until cooked through. Place the burgers in the buns and serve immediately.

STEP 1

STEP 2

WHY NOT ALSO MAKE YOUR OWN HAMBURGER BUNS. THEY WOULD BE SURE TO IMPRESS—PLUS YOU CAN'T BEAT THE SMELL OF FRESHLY BAKED BREAD!

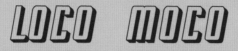

LOCO MOCO

PREP TIME: *20 minutes*   **COOK TIME:** *35 minutes*

THIS CROSS-CULTURAL HAWAIIAN SPECIALTY OF ASIAN RICE TOPPED WITH A BURGER AND A FRIED EGG, ALL SMOTHERED WITH GRAVY, IS OFTEN ENJOYED AS A POST-SURF BREAKFAST.

MAKES 4

1½ cups medium-grain rice
1 tablespoon butter, plus extra for grilling
1 tablespoon all-purpose flour
2 cups beef broth
1 pound fresh ground beef
4 eggs
salt and pepper

1. Cook the rice according to the package directions. Keep warm.

2. Melt the butter in a medium skillet over medium-low heat. Beat in the flour, then cook, stirring, for 4 minutes, until lightly browned. Beat in the broth, bring to simmering point, and simmer for 20 minutes, until thickened. Season with salt and pepper and keep warm.

3. Meanwhile, put the beef into a medium bowl and lightly season with salt and pepper, then divide into four equal portions and form each portion into a patty.

4. Add enough butter to a skillet to coat the bottom of the pan and melt over medium-high heat. Add the patties to the pan and cook for 4 minutes on each side, or until cooked to your liking. Remove from the pan and keep warm. Add the eggs to the pan and sprinkle with salt and pepper. Cook for about 3-4 minutes, until the whites are set and the yolks are beginning to set at the edges.

5. Divide the rice among four plates and top each portion with a burger, an egg, and plenty of gravy. Serve immediately.

STEP 1

STEP 2

STEP 4

THIS IS CERTAINLY A DIFFERENT BURGER DISH TO TRY. BECAUSE OF ITS UNUSUAL COMBINATION OF INGREDIENTS, YOU CAN ENJOY AT ANY TIME—FOR BREAKFAST, LUNCH, OR DINNER.

CHILI-GARLIC SAUCE BURGER

PREP TIME: *20 minutes, plus chilling*   **COOK TIME:** *20 minutes*

A MIXTURE OF BEEF AND PORK HELP MAKE THESE SPICY BURGERS DISTINCTIVE AND DELICIOUS.

MAKES 4

large bunch fresh cilantro

1 garlic clove

8 ounces fresh ground beef

8 ounces fresh ground pork

2 tablespoons red chili sauce

2 teaspoons finely grated ginger

2 teaspoons soy sauce

2 small bok choy

2 teaspoons vegetable oil

4 soft hamburger buns, halved

1. Finely chop half of the cilantro leaves. Finely chop the garlic.

2. Put the beef, pork, chili sauce, ginger, soy sauce, garlic, and chopped cilantro into a large bowl and mix to combine. Divide the mixture into four equal portions and shape each portion into a 1/2–3/4-inch-thick patty. Cover and chill in the refrigerator.

3. Coarsely chop the bok choy, discarding the thick ends. Heat a large skillet over high heat and add the oil, swirling to cover the bottom of the skillet. Add the bok choy and cook, stirring frequently, until wilted. Remove from the skillet and set aside.

4. Place the patties in the skillet and cook for about 4 minutes, until brown. Turn and cook for an additional 4 minutes, until they are cooked through and brown on both sides.

5. Place the burgers in the buns. Top each burger with some sautéed bok choy and the remaining whole cilantro leaves. Serve immediately.

THIS IS THE PERFECT BURGER FOR CHILE LOVERS EVERYWHERE. JUST REDUCE THE AMOUNT OF CHILI SAUCE USED IF YOU PREFER A MILDER TASTE.

PONZU MAYO TURKEY BURGER

PREP TIME: *20 minutes*   **COOK TIME:** *10 minutes*

A COMBINATION OF YUZU (A JAPANESE CITRUS FRUIT), BONITO FLAKES, SEAWEED, MIRIN, AND SOY SAUCE, PONZU SAUCE HAS ALL THE RIGHT FLAVORS ROLLED INTO ONE BOTTLE TO GARNISH THESE DELICIOUS, JUICY BURGERS.

MAKES 4

1 pound fresh ground turkey

2 tablespoons sesame seeds

4 teaspoons soy sauce, plus extra to serve

1 teaspoon toasted sesame oil

1 teaspoon minced garlic

¼ cup mayonnaise

2 tablespoons ponzu sauce

4 sesame seed hamburger buns, halved

1 cup baby salad greens

tomato slices

pepper

1. Put the turkey into a medium bowl with the sesame seeds, soy sauce, oil, and garlic, season with pepper, and gently mix to combine. Divide into four equal portions and form each portion into a patty. Place the patties on a large baking sheet.

2. Preheat the broiler to high and place the rack below the heat. Place the patties on the rack and broil for 5 minutes, then turn and continue cooking for an additional 4-5 minutes, until cooked through.

3. Combine the mayonnaise and ponzu sauce in a small bowl (the mixture will be thin). Coat each cut side of the buns with the sauce, then add the burgers. Top with some lettuce leaves and tomato slices, then sprinkle with pepper and a drizzle of soy sauce. Serve immediately.

STEP 1

STEP 3

YOU CAN BUY PONZU SAUCE FROM ASIAN GROCERY STORES. ALTERNATIVELY, BUY IT ONLINE.

BEEF TERIYAKI BURGER

PREP TIME: 10 minutes, plus chilling   **COOK TIME:** 10-15 minutes

MAKES 4

1 pound ground beef

8 scallions

2-4 garlic cloves

1-inch piece fresh ginger, grated

½ teaspoon wasabi or freshly grated horseradish, or to taste

3 teaspoons teriyaki sauce or marinade

2 teaspoons peanut oil

2 carrots, grated

1 cup shredded bok choy

½ cup shredded cucumber

4 soft hamburger buns, halved

crispy fried seaweed, to garnish (optional)

1. Place the ground beef, scallions, garlic, ginger, wasabi, and the teriyaki sauce in a food processor or blender and, using the pulse button, blend together. Shape into four equal patties, then cover and let chill in the refrigerator for 30 minutes.

2. Heat a heavy skillet and add 1 teaspoon of the oil. When hot, add the patties and cook over medium heat for 3-5 minutes on each side or until cooked to your liking. Add more oil if necessary. Keep warm.

3. Spoon a little of the vegetables onto the bun bottoms and top with the burgers and seaweed, if using. Add the bun lids and serve immediately.

A BLEND OF SOY SAUCE, WINE, VINEGAR, VARIOUS SPICES, AND A HINT OF SWEETNESS, TERIYAKI SAUCE IS USED AS A MARINADE TO TENDERIZE THE BEEF AND STEEP IT WITH SOME ASIAN FLAVORS.

CHAPTER 4
THE AWESOME SIDESHOW

HOMEMADE KETCHUP

PREP TIME: 10 minutes

COOK TIME: 15-20 minutes

KETCHUP IS AN IMMENSELY POPULAR STAPLE INGREDIENT,
BUT MANY PEOPLE NEVER THINK ABOUT MAKING THEIR OWN.
THIS RECIPE IS SIMPLE AND THE RESULTS ARE DELICIOUS.

MAKES ABOUT 1 CUP

2 tablespoons olive oil

1 red onion, peeled and chopped

2 garlic cloves, chopped

4 plum tomatoes, chopped

1 cup canned diced tomatoes

½ teaspoon ground ginger

½ teaspoon chili powder

3 tablespoons dark brown sugar

½ cup red wine vinegar

salt and pepper

1. Heat the olive oil in a large saucepan and add the onion, garlic, and all the tomatoes. Add the ginger and chili powder and season with salt and pepper. Cook for 15 minutes, or until soft.

2. Pour the mixture into a food processor or blender and blend well. Strain thoroughly to remove all the seeds. Return the mixture to the pan and add the sugar and vinegar. Return to a boil and cook until it is the consistency of ketchup.

3. Let cool then ladle into a sterilized jar (see page 199), and store in the refrigerator for up to 1 month.

STEP 1

STEP 2

IF YOU WANT TO CAN
ANY OF THESE CONDIMENTS OR
RELISHES, MAKE SURE YOU ALWAYS
USE CANNING JARS, AND FOLLOW
THE BOILING WATER CANNER'S
INSTRUCTIONS FOR STERILIZING
THE JARS AND LIDS BEFORE USE,
AND FOR STERILIZING THE
CONTENTS IN A WATER BATH.

BARBECUE SAUCE

PREP TIME: 15 minutes   COOK TIME: 20 minutes

MAKES ABOUT 1 CUP

1 tablespoon olive oil

1 small onion, finely chopped

2-3 garlic cloves, crushed

1 fresh red jalapeño chile, seeded and finely chopped (optional)

2 teaspoons tomato paste

1 teaspoon (or to taste) dry mustard

1 tablespoon red wine vinegar

1 tablespoon Worcestershire sauce

2-3 teaspoons brown sugar

1¼ cups water

1. Heat the oil in a small, heavy saucepan, add the onion, garlic, and chile, if using, and gently sauté, stirring frequently, for 3 minutes, or until beginning to soften. Remove from the heat.

2. Blend the tomato paste with the mustard, vinegar, and Worcestershire sauce to a paste, then stir into the onion mixture with 2 teaspoons of the sugar. Mix well, then gradually stir in the water.

3. Return to the heat and bring to a boil, stirring frequently. Reduce the heat and gently simmer, stirring occasionally, for 15 minutes. Taste and add the remaining sugar, if liked. Strain, if preferred, and serve hot or let cool and serve cold. It will keep in the refrigerator, in a sterilized jar (see page 199), for up to 2 weeks.

KA-BOOM!!

POW!

BARBECUE SAUCE IS THE ULTIMATE BURGER ACCOMPANIMENT AND TURNS THE AVERAGE BURGER INTO SOMETHING EXTRA SPECIAL.

HOMEMADE MUSTARD

PREP TIME: *15 minutes plus developing* **COOK TIME:** *no cooking*

LIKE A SPICY COUNTRY-STYLE DIJON MUSTARD, THE FLAVOR IMPROVES AND BECOMES LESS SPICY AFTER A COUPLE OF DAYS IN THE REFRIGERATOR.

MAKES ¾ CUP

3 tablespoons brown mustard seeds

3 tablespoons apple cider vinegar

1–2 tablespoons water

3 tablespoons dry mustard

2 teaspoons salt

2 teaspoons honey

1. Put the mustard seeds into a small, nonmetallic container with the vinegar and enough water to cover completely. Set aside for two days, covered, at room temperature.

2. Strain the mustard seeds, reserving the liquid. Grind in a spice grinder until some seeds are still whole while some are ground. You may have to push the seeds down and grind again, but the more you grind, the spicier the mustard will be.

3. Place the mixture in a small bowl with the dry mustard, salt, and honey. Add the reserved vinegar water and stir.

4. Place in a nonreactive, sterilized container (see page 199), and refrigerate for at least 2 days before serving. Use within 2 weeks.

STEP 1

STEP 2

STEP 3

THE PLEASING HEAT OF MUSTARD ILLUSTRATES ITS ABILITY TO STIMULATE THE CIRCULATION, SO THAT YOUTH-GIVING NUTRIENTS AND OXYGEN ARE DISTRIBUTED TO ALL PARTS OF THE BODY.

COLESLAW

PREP TIME: 10 minutes, plus chilling   COOK TIME: no cooking

COLESLAW IS A SUMMER PARTY STAPLE. IT WORKS PERFECTLY AS PART OF A SALAD, A BURGER TOPPING, OR SIMPLY ON ITS OWN.

SERVES 10—12

2/3 cup mayonnaise
2/3 cup plain yogurt
dash of Tabasco sauce
1 head green cabbage
4 carrots
1 green bell pepper
salt and pepper

1. To make the dressing, put the mayonnaise, yogurt, and Tabasco sauce into a small bowl, season with salt and pepper, and mix together. Chill in the refrigerator until required.

2. Cut the cabbage in half and then into quarters. Remove and discard the tough core. Finely shred the cabbage leaves. Peel the carrots and coarsely shred in a food processor or on a mandoline. Quarter and seed the bell pepper and cut the flesh into thin strips.

3. Mix together the vegetables in a large serving bowl and toss to mix. Pour the dressing over the vegetables and toss until well coated. Cover and chill in the refrigerator until required. Use within 2 days.

THERE ARE MANY GREAT ADD-ONS TO THIS POPULAR DISH. YOU CAN TRY NUTS, SEEDS, APPLE, RAISINS, AND CAPERS. CHEESE ALSO ADDS A GREAT TWIST.

HOMEMADE PICKLE RELISH

PREP TIME: *15 minutes, plus chilling*   **COOK TIME:** *20 minutes*

THIS RELISH LIGHTLY PICKLES THE CUCUMBERS AS PART OF THE PROCESS OF MAKING THE RELISH, GIVING IT A BRIGHT, FRESH FLAVOR.

MAKES 2 PINTS

4 cucumbers
1½ cups cider vinegar
1 teaspoon mustard seeds
1 teaspoon coriander seeds
¼ cup sugar
2 teaspoons salt
1 green bell pepper
1 small white onion

1. Trim the ends of the cucumbers, cut them in half lengthwise, seed, and finely chop.

2. Bring the vinegar to a boil in a large saucepan. Add the cucumbers and cook for about 4 minutes, stirring frequently, until they are just starting to lose their color and are tender but still crunchy.

3. Use a slotted spoon to scoop the cucumbers out of the vinegar and set them aside. Add the mustard seeds and coriander seeds to the vinegar and bring back to a boil. Stir in the sugar and salt and reduce the heat to simmering. Cook until the vinegar mixture is reduced to ½ cup.

4. Meanwhile, finely chop the green bell pepper and the onion. Mix with the cooked cucumber. Pour the vinegar over the vegetables and stir to combine. Transfer the relish to sterilized jars (see page 199). Cover and chill in the refrigerator for at least 1 hour before serving. It will keep in the refrigerator for up to 2 weeks.

STEP 4

STEP 1

This relish provides a great bite to any burger. The canning jar is a fun way to serve the pickles. Follow manufacturer's instructions for a boiling water canner if you want to can the pickles for long-term storage.

179

CHIPOTLE KETCHUP & CHIPOTLE MUSTARD

KETCHUP PREP TIME: *5 minutes*   **KETCHUP COOK TIME:** *8-10 minutes*
MUSTARD PREP TIME: *under 5 minutes*   **MUSTARD COOK TIME:** *no cooking*

WHY NOT ADD A SPECIAL SPICY KICK TO YOUR FAVORITE BURGER TOPPINGS? THESE RECIPES ARE SO EASY BUT ARE SURE TO ALWAYS IMPRESS.

MAKES 1 CUP

CHIPOTLE KETCHUP

1 cup prepared ketchup

½ teaspoon Worcestershire sauce

½ teaspoon light brown sugar

1 tablespoon fresh lemon juice, or to taste

1½ teaspoons chipotle powder, or to taste

1 teaspoon ground cumin

½ teaspoon ground turmeric

¼ teaspoon ground ginger

salt

CHIPOTLE MUSTARD

½ cup Dijon mustard

1 teaspoon chipotle powder, or to taste

1. For the ketchup, combine all the ingredients in a small saucepan, season with salt, and place over medium heat. Bring to a simmer and cook, stirring frequently, for 5 minutes, or until the ketchup is slightly thickened. Remove from the heat and let cool. Transfer to a sterilized jar (see page 199), and refrigerate for up to 2 weeks.

2. To make the chipotle mustard, place the ingredients in a small bowl and stir to thoroughly combine. Transfer to a sterilized jar (see page 199), and refrigerate for up to 2 weeks.

KA-BOOM!!

CHIPOTLE IS A DRIED, SMOKED JALEPEÑO — IT IS USED FREQUENTLY IN MEXICAN COOKING AND ADDS A GREAT, DISTINCTIVE SMOKY FLAVOR TO ANY DISH.

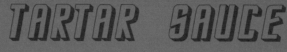

TARTAR SAUCE

PREP TIME: *10 minutes, plus chilling*   **COOK TIME:** *no cooking*

TARTAR SAUCE IS DELICIOUS ON ALMOST ANY
SEAFOOD-BASED BURGER, INCLUDING CLASSIC FISH
BURGER (SEE PAGE 58).

MAKES ABOUT 1 CUP

2 small gherkin pickles

1 scallion

1 tablespoon capers

handful of fresh
flat-leaf parsley

¾ cup mayonnaise

1 tablespoon
lemon juice

salt and pepper

1. Finely chop the pickles, scallion, capers, and parsley. Put them into a small bowl and stir in the mayonnaise.

2. Add the lemon juice and stir, then season with salt and pepper. Cover and chill in the refrigerator for at least 30 minutes or up to 2 days before serving.

FOR A MORE UNUSUAL TWIST
TO THIS CLASSIC FISH SAUCE,
ADD EITHER SOME CHOPPED
HARD-BOILED EGGS OR
OLIVES—OR BOTH!

TOMATO & RED ONION RELISH

SERVES 4

OVEN-DRIED TOMATOES

8 ripe tomatoes

1–2 tablespoons virgin olive oil

salt and pepper

SAUCE

1 tablespoon virgin olive oil

2 large red onions, thinly sliced

2 cups arugula or baby spinach leaves

1. For the oven-dried tomatoes, preheat the oven to 300°F. Cut the tomatoes in half, and arrange all the halves in a large roasting pan. Drizzle with the oil and season with salt and pepper. Cook in the oven for $1\frac{1}{4}$–$1\frac{1}{2}$ hours, or until roasted but still moist.

2. For the sauce, heat the oil in a large skillet. Add the onions and sauté over low heat until soft and golden brown. Place eight of the oven-dried tomatoes in a food processor or blender and process until pureed. Add to the onions in the skillet.

3. Slice the remaining eight tomato halves and add to the skillet with the arugula. Season with salt and pepper and cook until the leaves have just wilted. Serve immediately.

STEP 1

STEP 2

STEP 3

THIS RECIPE IS PERFECT IF YOU GROW YOUR OWN TOMATOES. WHETHER THEY'RE FROM YOUR GARDEN OR STORE-BOUGHT, MAKE SURE THEY'RE THE RIPEST YOU CAN FIND.

GUACAMOLE

PREP TIME: *15 minutes, plus chilling*

COOK TIME: *no cooking*

SERVES 4

1 ripe tomato

2 limes

2-3 ripe small to medium avocados, or 1-2 large ones

¼-½ onion, finely chopped

pinch of ground cumin

pinch of mild chili powder

½-1 fresh green chile, such as jalapeño or serrano, seeded and finely chopped

1 tablespoon finely chopped fresh cilantro leaves, plus extra to garnish

1. Place the tomato in a heatproof bowl, pour over enough boiling water to cover, and let stand for 30 seconds. Drain and plunge into cold water. Peel off the skin. Cut the tomato in half, seed, and chop the flesh.

2. Squeeze the juice from the limes into a small bowl. Cut 1 avocado in half around the pit. Twist the two halves apart in opposite directions, then remove the pit with the tip a sharp knife. Carefully peel off the skin, dice the flesh, and toss in the bowl of lime juice to prevent the flesh from discoloring. Repeat with the remaining avocados. Mash the avocados coarsely with a fork.

3. Add the onion, tomato, cumin, chili powder, chiles, and cilantro to the avocados and mix together gently. Press a sheet of plastic wrap over the surface of the guacamole to prevent discoloration, then chill in the refrigerator until ready to serve. Use within 1-2 days.

KA-POW!

A GOOD GUACAMOLE ALWAYS DEPENDS ON USING QUALITY, RIPE AVOCADOS. MASHING INSTEAD OF PUREEING GIVES CONTROL OVER THE TEXTURE.

MAYONNAISE

PREP TIME: 5 minutes   COOK TIME: no cooking

ONE OF THE BASIC SAUCES IN THE FRENCH REPERTOIRE,
HOMEMADE MAYONNAISE HAS A MILDER FLAVOR
THAN MOST COMMERCIAL VARIETIES.

MAKES ABOUT 1¼ CUPS

2 extra-large egg yolks

2 teaspoons Dijon mustard

¾ teaspoon salt, or to taste

2 tablespoons lemon juice or white wine vinegar, plus extra if needed

about 1¼ cups sunflower oil

white pepper

1. Process the egg yolks with the Dijon mustard, salt, and white pepper to taste in a food processor, blender, or by hand. Add the lemon juice and process again.

2. With the motor still running, add the oil, drop by drop at first. When the sauce begins to thicken, the oil can then be added in a slow, steady stream. Taste and adjust the seasoning with extra salt, pepper, and lemon juice, if necessary. If the sauce seems too thick, slowly add 1 tablespoon of hot water or lemon juice.

3. Use at once or store in a sterilized jar (see page 199) in the refrigerator and use within 1 week.

A GREAT TIP FOR MAKING MAYONNAISE IS TO REMOVE THE EGGS FROM THE REFRIGERATOR IN ORDER TO BRING THEM BACK TO ROOM TEMPERATURE BEFORE USING. THIS WILL PREVENT THE MIXTURE FROM SPLITTING.

CHOW CHOW (CORN RELISH)

PREP TIME: *20 minutes, plus cooling*   **COOK TIME:** *20 minutes*

THIS RELISH MAKES THE PLAINEST BURGER A TREAT, AND IS ESPECIALLY DELICIOUS ON SHRIMP-CHIVE BURGERS (SEE PAGE 150).

MAKES 2 PINTS

3 corn cobs
1 red bell pepper
1 jalapeño chile
½ cup cider vinegar
½ cup light brown sugar
1 tablespoon salt
1 tablespoon mustard seeds
½ teaspoon celery seeds
1 red onion, diced

1. Cut the kernels off the corn cobs. Seed and dice the red bell pepper and the chile.

2. Put the corn, red bell pepper, chile, vinegar, sugar, salt, mustard seeds, and celery seeds into a large saucepan over medium-high heat and bring to a boil. Reduce the heat to simmering and cook, stirring occasionally, for about 15 minutes, until the mixture reduces slightly. The sugar will melt, producing enough liquid to cover the vegetables.

3. Stir the onions into the corn mixture and remove from the heat. Let cool, then ladle the relish into a sterilized jar (see page 199), and refrigerate for up to 1 month.

STEP 2

STEP 1

THIS TASTY RELISH LOOKS
ATTRACTIVE SERVED IN A
CANNING JAR. FOR LONG-TERM
STORAGE IN A CANNING JAR, USE
A BOILING WATER CANNER,
FOLLOWING THE MANUFACTURER'S
INSTRUCTIONS.

AIOLI

PREP TIME: *10 minutes, plus chilling*

COOK TIME: *no cooking*

THIS IS A FAMOUS FRENCH GARLIC MAYONNAISE FROM PROVENCE—DEFINITELY ONE FOR GARLIC LOVERS!

SERVES 4

3 large garlic cloves, minced

2 egg yolks

1 cup extra virgin olive oil

1 tablespoon lemon juice

1 tablespoon lime juice

1 tablespoon Dijon mustard

1 tablespoon chopped fresh tarragon

salt and pepper

fresh tarragon sprig, to garnish

1. Make sure that all the ingredients are at room temperature. Place the garlic and egg yolks in a food processor or blender and process until well blended. With the motor running, pour the oil, teaspoon by teaspoon, through the feeder tube until the mixture starts to thicken, then pour in the remaining oil in a thin stream until a thick mayonnaise forms.

2. Add the lemon juice, lime juice, mustard, and tarragon and season with salt and pepper. Blend until smooth, then transfer to a nonmetallic bowl. Garnish with a tarragon sprig.

3. Store in the refrigerator, covered, until needed, for up to 2 days.

GARLIC'S TRADITIONAL USE AS A
MEDICINAL PLANT IS DUE TO ITS
VARIOUS SULFUR COMPOUNDS,
WHICH WORK TO DETOXIFY,
CLEANSE, AND REPAIR CELLS TO
HELP YOU LOOK AND FEEL YOUNG.

BEEF CHILI

PREP TIME: *20 minutes*   **COOK TIME:** *1 hour*

THIS THICK, DELICIOUS CHILI IS MADE TO GO ON
TOP OF CHILI BURGERS (SEE PAGE 36),
OR IT CAN BE SERVED ON ITS OWN.

(SEE PAGE 36)

MAKES ENOUGH TOPPING FOR 8–10 BURGERS

2 tablespoons olive oil
1 onion, chopped
1 red bell pepper, diced
3 garlic cloves, minced
1 pound fresh ground beef
2 tablespoons chili powder
½ teaspoon cayenne pepper
1 (14½-ounce) can diced tomatoes
1¾ cups water
2 tablespoons chopped fresh parsley
salt and pepper

1. Heat 1 tablespoon of the oil in a large, heavy saucepan over medium heat. Add the onion, red bell pepper, and garlic and sauté for about 5 minutes, stirring, until tender. Remove the sautéed vegetables from the pan, then add the remaining oil.

2. When hot, add the ground beef with the chili powder and cayenne pepper, and season with salt and pepper. Stir to coat the meat with the spices and sauté for about 10 minutes, stirring frequently and breaking up the meat with a wooden spoon, until brown.

3. Add the sautéed vegetables, the tomatoes with their can juices, and the water to the pan. Bring to a boil, reduce the heat, and simmer for about 45 minutes, stirring occasionally, until the sauce is thick. Season with salt and pepper and stir in the parsley.

4. Serve immediately or let cool and store in the refrigerator, covered, for up to 4 days before using.

STEP 1

STEP 2

STEP 3

FOR A BIT OF ADDED INDULGENCE, TOP THE BEEF CHILI WITH SOME GRATED CHEDDAR CHEESE—DELICIOUS!

QUICK PICKLED ONIONS

PREP TIME: *15 minutes, plus chilling*   **COOK TIME:** *no cooking*

These sweet, spicy, and tangy onions require no heating, so they're easy to make anytime. Include them at the table with all your standard burger condiments.

MAKES ABOUT 2 CUPS

1 cup distilled white vinegar

½ cup sugar

1 teaspoon chipotle powder, or to taste

2 medium red onions, cut into rings

salt

1. In a medium bowl, combine the vinegar, sugar, chipotle powder, and salt to taste. Beat to dissolve the sugar.

2. Place the onions in a heavy-duty, zip-top bag and pour the marinade over the onions. Toss to coat. Cover and refrigerate for 30 minutes, moving the mixture around a couple of times to evenly distribute the marinade. Drain before serving. Store in an airtight container in the refrigerator for up to 2 days.

THE ONION IS A TOP HEALTH FOOD, CONTAINING SULFUR COMPOUNDS THAT ARE NATURAL ANTIBIOTICS OFFERING PROTECTION FROM CANCERS AND HEART DISEASE.

PICKLED JALAPEÑOS

PREP TIME: 15 minutes, plus cooling

COOK TIME: 15 minutes

THESE JALAPEÑOS ARE A SIMPLE VERSION OF ESCABECHE, PERFECT FOR GIVING BURGERS A LITTLE EXTRA KICK.

MAKES 2 PINTS

1 pound jalapeño chiles
1 white onion
8 garlic cloves
3 cups apple cider vinegar or white distilled vinegar
2 tablespoons salt
2 bay leaves
2 teaspoons sugar

1. Remove the stems from the jalapeños and cut the chiles into thick rings.

2. Peel and coarsely chop the onion. Peel the garlic cloves.

3. Bring the vinegar, salt, bay leaves, and sugar to a boil in a large saucepan. Add the chiles, onions, and garlic. Reduce the heat to simmering and cook for about 5 minutes, until the chiles are tender.

4. Ladle the chiles, onions, and garlic into sterilized jars (see right), leaving a 1-inch gap at the top. Fill with the vinegar to completely cover, then let cool to room temperature. Place a circle of wax paper or plastic wrap on top, seal tightly with the covers, and store in the refrigerator for up to 2 months.

To sterilize jars and lids, wash in hot soapy water, rinse well, and put on a rack in a big kettle. Fill with hot water to 1–2 inches above the jars, cover, bring to a boil, and boil for 10 minutes (add 1 minute per 1,000 feet at high altitudes). Let sit in the water until ready to use.

THE PERFECT BURGER BUN

PREP TIME: 20 minutes, plus resting

COOK TIME: 15-20 minutes

MAKES 8 BUNS

3¹⁄₃ cups white bread flour, plus extra for dusting

1½ teaspoons salt

2 teaspoons superfine sugar

1 teaspoon active dry yeast

²⁄₃ cup lukewarm water

²⁄₃ cup lukewarm milk

vegetable oil, for brushing

2-3 tablespoons sesame seeds

1. Sift together the flour and salt into a bowl and stir in the sugar and yeast. Make a well in the center and pour in the lukewarm water and milk. Stir well with a wooden spoon until the dough begins to come together, then knead with your hands until it leaves the side of the bowl. Turn out onto a lightly floured surface and knead well for about 10 minutes, until smooth and elastic.

2. Brush a bowl with oil. Shape the dough into a ball, put it in the bowl, and put the bowl into a plastic bag or cover with a damp dish towel. Let rise in a warm place for 1 hour, until the dough has doubled in volume.

3. Brush two baking sheets with oil. Invert the dough onto a lightly floured surface and punch down by pushing into the dough with your fist. Divide it into eight equal pieces, shape each into a ball, and put them on the prepared baking sheets. Flatten slightly with a lightly floured hand and put the baking sheets into plastic bags or cover with damp dish towels. Let rise in a warm place for 30 minutes.

4. Preheat the oven to 400°F. Lightly press the center of each bun with your fingers to release any large air bubbles. Brush the tops with the oil and sprinkle with sesame seeds. Bake for 15-20 minutes, until light golden brown. Transfer to wire racks to cool.

CARAMELIZED ONIONS

PREP TIME: 5 minutes

COOK TIME: 25 minutes

SLICED ONIONS, COOKED SLOWLY UNTIL GOLDEN BROWN
AND SLIGHTLY SWEET, ARE A DELICIOUS ACCOMPANIMENT
TO ALL KINDS OF BURGERS.

SERVES 4–6

1-2 tablespoons
vegetable oil or olive oil

½ red onion, sliced

½ teaspoon finely
chopped fresh
rosemary, thyme or
oregano (optional)

½ teaspoon red wine
vinegar

salt and pepper

1. Heat enough oil to coat the bottom of a large skillet over medium heat until shimmering. Add the onion and cook on one side for 3 minutes, until brown. Add the herbs, if using, stir, and continue cooking, stirring occasionally, for about 12 minutes, until nicely browned.

2. Season with salt and pepper. Add the vinegar and cook for an additional 8-10 minutes, until very soft.

3. Serve immediately, or let cool and store in an airtight container in the refrigerator for up to 3 days.

STEP 1

STEP 2

CARAMELIZED ONIONS
ARE BOTH RICH AND SWEET.
THEY REQUIRE VERY LITTLE
ATTENTION AND ARE EASY
TO COOK, MAKING THEM THE
PERFECT BURGER TOPPING.

CRISPY ONION RINGS

PREP TIME: *15 minutes*   **COOK TIME:** *15 minutes*

SERVES 4-6

1 cup all-purpose flour
pinch of salt
1 egg
2/3 cup low-fat milk
4 large onions
vegetable oil, for deep-frying
chili powder, to taste (optional)
salt and pepper
lettuce leaves, to serve

1. To make the batter, sift the flour and a pinch of salt into a large bowl and make a well in the center. Break the egg into the well and gently beat with a whisk. Gradually whisk in the milk, drawing the flour from the side into the liquid in the center to form a smooth batter.

2. Leaving the onions whole, slice widthwise into 1/4-inch slices, then separate each slice into rings.

3. Heat the oil in a deep-fat fryer or deep, heavy saucepan to 350–375°F, or until a cube of bread browns in 30 seconds.

4. Using the tines of a fork, pick up several onions rings at a time and dip in the batter. Let any excess batter drip off, then add the onions to the oil and deep-fry for 1–2 minutes until they rise to the surface of the oil and become crisp and golden brown. Remove from the oil, drain on paper towels, and keep warm while deep-frying the remaining onion rings in batches. Do not try to deep-fry too many at a time, because this will reduce the temperature of the oil and the onion rings will absorb some of the oil and become soggy.

5. Season the onion rings with chili powder, if desired, and salt and pepper, then serve immediately on a bed of lettuce leaves.

There are dozens of different methods that people claim can help to prevent you from crying while cutting onions, such as leaving the root intact until the very end, peeling them under running water, chilling them before cutting, and even whistling while you work!

FRIES

SERVES 4

3 large russet potatoes
sunflower, corn, or peanut oil, for deep-frying
salt and pepper

1. Peel the potatoes and cut into even ½-inch sticks. As soon as they are prepared, put them into a large bowl of cold water to prevent discoloration, then let them soak for 30 minutes to remove the excess starch.

2. Drain the potatoes and dry well on a clean dish towel. Heat the oil in a deep-fat fryer or large, heavy saucepan to 375°F. If you do not have a thermometer, test the temperature by dropping a potato stick into the oil. If it sinks, the oil isn't hot enough; if it floats and the oil bubbles around the potato, it is ready. Carefully add a small batch of potatoes to the oil (this is to be sure of even cooking and to avoid reducing the temperature of the oil) and deep-fry for 5-6 minutes, until soft but not browned. Remove from the oil and drain well on paper towels. Let cool for at least 5 minutes. Continue to deep-fry the remaining potatoes in the same way, letting the oil return to the correct temperature each time.

3. When ready to serve, reheat the oil to 400°F. Add the potatoes, in small batches, and deep-fry for 2-3 minutes, until golden brown. Remove from the oil and drain on paper towels. Serve immediately, seasoned with salt and pepper.

French fries, pommes frites, or chips, from chunky to shoe-string—call them what you want, but any burger—from the most simple to gourmet, wouldn't be the same without this classic accompaniment.

POTATO SALAD

PREP TIME: *30 minutes,*
plus chilling

COOK TIME: *30 minutes*

COOL AND CREAMY, THIS SALAD SHOULD BE AN INTEGRAL PART OF ANY BARBECUE.

SERVES 8

2¾ pounds white round, Yellow Finn, or new potatoes

½ cup mayonnaise

¼ cup sour cream

⅓ cup white wine vinegar

1 teaspoon whole-grain mustard

½ teaspoon dried dill

½ red onion, finely chopped

1 celery stalk, finely chopped

¼ cup chopped gherkin pickles

¼ cup chopped roasted red pepper

2 hard-boiled eggs, chopped (optional)

salt and pepper

1. Place the unpeeled potatoes in a medium saucepan and cover with lightly salted water. Bring to a boil over high heat, then reduce the heat and simmer for 20–30 minutes, until fork-tender.

2. Put the mayonnaise, sour cream, vinegar, mustard, and dill into a bowl, season with salt and pepper, and mix together.

3. Drain the potatoes and let cool slightly, then slip off the skins with your fingers or with a paring knife. Chop the potatoes into ½-inch pieces and add to the dressing while still warm. Stir in the onion, celery, pickles, roasted pepper, and egg, if using. Cover and chill for at least 2 hours or overnight. Use within 1–2 days.

STEP 3

STEP 1

One of the most popular add-ons to this BBQ staple is hard-boiled eggs. Simply hard boil three eggs and chop before adding to the bowl with the rest of the ingredients.

MACARONI SALAD

PREP TIME: *30 minutes, plus chilling*

COOK TIME: *10 minutes*

THIS CLASSIC SALAD IS AN ESSENTIAL PART OF PICNICS AND GOES WELL WITH A JUICY BURGER.

SERVES 6–8

8 ounces dried elbow macaroni

¼ cup mayonnaise, plus extra if needed

¼ cup plain yogurt

1 tablespoon fresh lemon juice

½ teaspoon garlic salt

¼ teaspoon pepper

1 stalk celery, diced

3 scallions, finely chopped

¼ cup finely chopped ripe black olives

½ tomato, finely chopped

2 tablespoons chopped fresh flat-leaf parsley

salt and pepper

1. Bring a medium saucepan of lightly salted water to a boil, add the macaroni, and cook according to the package directions. Drain.

2. Meanwhile, combine the mayonnaise, yogurt, lemon juice, garlic salt, and pepper in a large bowl. Stir in the hot macaroni, then add the celery, scallions, olives, tomatoes, and parsley. Season with salt and pepper and add more mayonnaise if it seems dry, then let cool completely.

3. Cover with plastic wrap and chill for at least 2 hours, until cold. Serve cold. The salad will keep in the refrigerator for up to 3 days.

THERE ARE MANY VARIATIONS OF THIS RECIPE FROM ALL OVER THE WORLD. THEY VARY WIDELY IN INGREDIENTS AND EVEN IN THE TEMPERATURE WHICH THE DISH IS SERVED.

FRESH LEMONADE

PREP TIME: 15 minutes, plus standing

COOK TIME: no cooking

THERE IS NOTHING MORE REFRESHING ON A HOT SUMMER'S DAY THAN A GLASS OR TWO OF HOMEMADE LEMONADE— THERE IS, OF COURSE, THE ADDED BONUS THAT THERE ARE NO ARTIFICIAL ADDITIVES.

SERVES 6

4 large lemons, preferably unwaxed
1 cup sugar
3½ cups boiling water
ice cubes

1. Scrub the lemons well, then dry. Using a vegetable peeler, peel three of the lemons thinly. Place the peel in a large heatproof bowl, add the sugar and boiling water, and stir well until the sugar has dissolved. Cover and let stand for at least 3 hours, stirring occasionally. Meanwhile, squeeze the juice from the 3 peeled lemons and reserve.

2. Remove and discard the lemon peel and stir in the reserved lemon juice. Thinly slice the remaining lemon and cut the slices in half. Add to the lemonade together with the ice cubes. Stir and serve immediately.

You can try using oranges or limes or a mixture of all three fruits for some equally refreshing thirst quenchers.

ORANGE & LIME ICED TEA

PREP TIME: 10 minutes, plus cooling

COOK TIME: less than 5 minutes

ICED TEA IS ALWAYS REFRESHING AND EVEN IF YOU ARE NOT A TEA DRINKER, THIS VERSION IS ESPECIALLY FRESH AND FRUITY. KEEP SOME IN THE REFRIGERATOR IF YOU DON'T DRINK IT ALL AT ONCE.

SERVES 2

1¼ cups water
2 tea bags
½ cup orange juice
¼ cup lime juice
1–2 tablespoons brown sugar
ice cubes

TO DECORATE

lime wedge
granulated sugar
orange or lime slices

1. Pour the water into a saucepan and bring to a boil. Remove from the heat, add the tea bags, and let steep for 5 minutes. Remove the tea bags and let the tea cool to room temperature. Transfer to a pitcher, cover with plastic wrap, and chill in the refrigerator for at least 45 minutes.

2. When the tea has chilled, pour in the orange juice and lime juice. Add sugar to taste.

3. Take two glasses and rub the rims with a lime wedge, then dip them in granulated sugar to frost. Put the ice cubes into the glasses and pour over the tea. Decorate with orange or lime slices and serve immediately.

KA-POW!

From soft drinks and beer to blended drinks, always offer a good choice at summer parties. Include plenty of bottled water on your shopping list, and place buckets filled with ice cubes at various points so guests can help themselves.

CLUB MOJITO

THIS TRADITIONAL CUBAN COCKTAIL HAS RECENTLY COME BACK INTO VOGUE. IMPRESS YOUR GUESTS WITH THIS REFRESHING, REVITALIZING AND DELICIOUS TREAT!

SERVES 1

1 teaspoon syrup de gomme
a few fresh mint leaves
juice of 1/2 lime
ice cubes
2 measures Jamaican rum
club soda
dash of Angostura bitters

1. Put the syrup, mint leaves, and lime juice in a glass and crush or muddle the mint leaves.

2. Add ice and the rum, then fill up with club soda. Finish with a dash of Angostura bitters. Serve immediately.

DARK RUM IS RICH IN FLAVOR AND REDOLENT OF VACATIONS-IN-THE-SUNSHINE MEMORIES ...

MARGARITA

THIS COCKTAIL, INVENTED IN 1942 IN MEXICO, IS A MORE CIVILIZED VERSION OF THE ORIGINAL WAY TO DRINK TEQUILA—A LICK OF SALT FROM THE BACK OF THE HAND, A SHOT OF TEQUILA, AND A SUCK OF LIME JUICE!

SERVES 1

lime wedges
coarse salt
3 measures white tequila
1 measure Triple Sec or Cointreau
2 measures lime juice
cracked ice

1. Rub the rim of a chilled cocktail glass with a lime wedge and then dip in a saucer of coarse salt to frost.

2. Shake the tequila, Triple Sec, and lime juice vigorously over cracked ice until well frosted.

3. Strain into the glass and dress with a lime wedge. Serve immediately.

This refreshing pick-me-up offers a classic combination of ingredients that make it unsurprising that it's one of the world's most popular cocktails.